Edexcel GCSE
RELIGIOUS STUDIES
RELIGION AND LIFE (UNIT 1) and RELIGION AND SOCIETY (UNIT 8)

my revision notes

Edexcel GCSE
RELIGIOUS STUDIES
RELIGION AND LIFE (UNIT 1) and RELIGION AND SOCIETY (UNIT 8)

Victor W. Watton

Every effort has been made to trace all copyright holders, but if any have been inadvertently overlooked the Publishers will be pleased to make the necessary arrangements at the first opportunity.

Although every effort has been made to ensure that website addresses are correct at time of going to press, Hodder Education cannot be held responsible for the content of any website mentioned in this book. It is sometimes possible to find a relocated web page by typing in the address of the home page for a website in the URL window of your browser.

Hachette UK's policy is to use papers that are natural, renewable and recyclable products and made from wood grown in sustainable forests. The logging and manufacturing processes are expected to conform to the environmental regulations of the country of origin.

Orders: please contact Bookpoint Ltd, 130 Milton Park, Abingdon, Oxon OX14 4SB. Telephone: +44 (0)1235 827720. Fax: +44 (0)1235 400454. Lines are open 9.00a.m.–5.00p.m., Monday to Saturday, with a 24-hour message answering service. Visit our website at www.hoddereducation.co.uk.

© Victor Watton 2014

First published in 2014 by
Hodder Education,
an Hachette UK company
London NW1 3BH

Impression number 10 9 8 7 6 5 4 3 2 1
Year 2018 2017 2016 2015 2014

Typeset in 12/14 Cronos Pro-Light by Datapage (India) Pvt. Ltd.
Printed and bound in India

A catalogue record for this title is available from the British Library
ISBN 9781471801396

Get the most from this book

This book will help you to revise for the Edexcel GCSE in Religious Studies specification. It is essential to review your work, learn it and test your understanding.

Tick each box when you have:

● revised and understood a topic

● tested yourself

● practised the exam questions and gone online to see the answer guidance.

☑ **Tick to track your progress**

Use the revision planner on pages iv–vi to plan your revision, topic by topic.

You can also keep track of your revision by ticking off each topic heading in the book. You may find it helpful to add your own notes as you work through each topic.

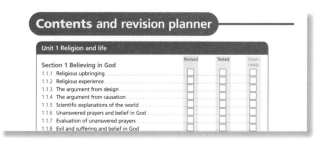

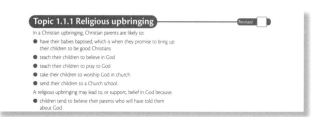

Features to help you succeed

Exam tips

Throughout the book there are tips to help you boost your final grade.

Common mistake

Identifies the typical mistakes candidates make and explains how you can avoid them.

Now test yourself

These short, knowledge-based questions provide the first step in testing your learning. Answers are provided at the back of the book.

Key terms

Clear, concise definitions of essential key terms are provided on the page where they first appear. You can also find them in the Glossary at the back of the book.

Exam practice

Practice exam questions are provided for each section. Use them to consolidate your revision and practise your exam skills.

Online

Go online to see revision notes for Units 1 and 8 on Judaism, Hinduism and Sikhism at **www.therevisionbutton.co.uk/myrevisionnotes**.

Contents and revision planner

Contents and revision planner

Introduction

What is GCSE Religious Studies about?

The course aims to:

- encourage candidates to think through some of the big issues that everyone faces in their adult lives
- enable candidates to explore religious and moral beliefs so that they can become more sure of their own beliefs and explain them clearly to others
- develop candidates' awareness of other people's beliefs and the nature of the society in which they live
- give candidates the understanding, knowledge and skills to enable them to live as responsible citizens in Britain's multi-ethnic, multi-faith society.

What is covered in GCSE Religious Studies?

Edexcel offers sixteen units for GCSE Religious Studies and candidates must study two of these to gain a full GCSE. This guide covers Unit 1 Religion and life based on a study of Christianity and at least one other religion, and Unit 8 Religion and society based on a study of Christianity and at least one other religion.

Each unit is divided into four sections. For Unit 1, these are:

- Believing in God
- Matters of life and death
- Marriage and the family
- Religion and community cohesion.

For Unit 8, they are:

- Rights and responsibilities
- Environmental and medical issues
- Peace and conflict
- Crime and punishment.

For each unit, you should revise all the topics in Section 1. In Sections 2, 3 and 4, for the topics which say 'one religion other than Christianity', you only need to revise **one religion** from Islam, Judaism, Hinduism or Sikhism.

If you have studied either Judaism, or Hinduism or Sikhism at school, you can find the revision notes for these on the website:
www.therevisionbutton.co.uk/myrevisionnotes

How does the assessment work?

Each unit has a separate exam lasting 1 hour 30 minutes. The exam paper is divided into four sections, with two questions on each section, and you are expected to answer one question from each section.

Each question has the same format:

● Part a) is a 2-mark question on the key terms – so you need to learn all the key terms and their meanings.

● Part b) is a 4-mark question asking what you think about one of the issues you have studied – so you need to say whether or not you agree and give two developed reasons for your opinion.

● Part c) is an 8-mark question testing your understanding by asking you to explain something – so you need to give four good reasons and use specialist vocabulary (the key terms and the specialist terms on pages 105–8).

● Part d) is a 6-mark question requiring you to evaluate a statement – so you need to say what your opinion is and give three reasons for your opinion, then you need to give three reasons why some people may disagree with you. Either your opinion, or the opposite one, must be religious with religious reasons.

Up to 4 marks will be awarded for your spelling, punctuation and grammar (SPAG) in your answer to Section 1 of both exam papers. This means you should take extra care with your spelling and make sure you use full stops and capital letters. You should use paragraphs if your answers to parts c) and/or d) are long.

How to deal with the exam paper

1   When you go into the exam hall and find your desk, your exam paper should be face up on the desk. Before you are allowed to open the paper, you can complete the front cover by:

   ● writing your surname in the first top box

   ● writing your first names in the adjoining box (if there is not enough room, write initials for names that will not fit)

   ● writing your centre number (this will be on display in the hall) in the first box below

   ● writing your personal exam number (you will receive this from your school before the exam) in the adjoining box.

   It is important that you get all of these completely correct, otherwise someone else may get your mark and grade!

2   When you are told to start, make a note of the time. You have 22 minutes per question (you could work on – part a) 2 minutes, part b) 4 minutes, part c) 9 minutes, part d) 7 minutes). You should try not to go beyond this as you will lose marks on Section 4 if you run out of time.

3   Start on Section 1 by choosing one of the questions – either the whole of question 1 (parts a, b, c, d) or the whole of question 2 (parts a, b, c, d). You should decide on which question to choose by whether you can do parts c) and d) as these are worth 14 marks of the 20 available.

4 Make sure you read the question carefully before you answer it and highlight key words such as why, how, some, others, choose one religion other than Christianity.

5 Make sure you put a line through the box beside the question you have chosen at the top of the first answer page. Your answers will be scanned and put onto a website, and the examiner will only be marking specific questions. If you do not indicate which question you have answered, your answer may not be marked.

6 Make sure that you use sentences, full stops, capital letters and paragraphs and take extra care with your spelling in your answers to Section 1.

7 If you run out of space, ask for a supplementary sheet of paper. The scanner does not pick up any writing outside the margins.

8 If you have any time left:

   ● check that you have answered every part of each question

   ● go through your answers to Section 1, and check the spelling (especially of key terms and specialist vocabulary) and punctuation (especially your use of full stops and capital letters)

   ● go through each part d) answer, checking that you have three reasons for each point of view and that at least one point of view is religious, and add extra reasons if necessary.

Countdown to my exams

6–8 weeks to go

- Start by looking at the specification available from **www.edexcel.com**. Make sure you know exactly what material you need to revise and the style of the examination. Use the revision planner on pages vi–viii to familiarise yourself with the topics.

- Organise your notes, making sure you have covered everything on the specification. The revision planner will help you group your notes into topics.

- Work out a realistic revision plan that will allow you time for relaxation. Set aside days and times for all the subjects that you need to study, and stick to your timetable.

- Set yourself sensible targets. Break your revision down into focused sessions of around 40 minutes, divided by breaks. These Revision Notes organise the basic facts into short, memorable sections to make revising easier.

Revised ☐

4–6 weeks to go

- Read through the relevant sections of this book and refer to the exam tips, common mistakes and key terms. Test your understanding of each topic by working through the 'Now test yourself' questions in the book and checking the answers at the back of the book.

- Make a note of any problem areas as you revise, and ask your teacher to go over these in class.

- Look at past papers. They are one of the best ways to revise and practise your exam skills. Write or prepare planned answers to the exam practice questions provided in this book.

- Try different revision methods. For example, you can make notes using mind maps, spider diagrams or flash cards.

- Track your progress using the revision planner and give yourself a reward when you have achieved your target.

Revised ☐

One week to go

- Try to fit in at least one more timed practice of an entire past paper and seek feedback from your teacher, comparing your work closely with the mark scheme.

- Check out the revision planner to make sure you haven't missed out any topics. Brush up on any areas of difficulty by talking them over with a friend or getting help from your teacher.

- Attend any revision classes put on by your teacher. Remember, he or she is an expert at preparing people for examinations.

Revised ☐

The day before the examination

- Flick through these Revision Notes for useful reminders, for example the exam tips, common mistakes and key terms.

- Check the time and place of your examination.

- Make sure you have everything you need – extra pens and pencils, tissues, a watch, bottled water, sweets.

- Allow some time to relax and have an early night to ensure you are fresh and alert for the examinations.

Revised ☐

My exam

Date: ....

Time: ....

Location: ....

Section 1 Believing in God

Topic 1.1.1 Religious upbringing

In a Christian upbringing, Christian parents are likely to:

- have their babies baptised, which is when they promise to bring up their children to be good Christians
- teach their children to believe in God
- teach their children to pray to God
- take their children to worship God in church
- send their children to a Church school.

A religious upbringing may lead to, or support, belief in God because:

- children tend to believe their parents who will have told them about God
- Christians pray to God; children will believe that God exists because their parents would not waste their time praying to nothing
- seeing so many people worshipping God when they go to church will make children believe God exists
- children will be taught that God exists when they go to Sunday school, or Church school, and will believe it because their teachers tell them it is true.

Evaluation of religious upbringing

1 Some people think a religious upbringing is a good thing because it:
   - helps to keep a family together as parents and children join together for religious activities
   - gives children an understanding of what is right and wrong, and gives them good morals
   - gives children a sense of belonging and community, giving them emotional stability.

2 Other people think a religious upbringing is a bad thing because it:
   - means children are brought up following a religion they have not chosen
   - can take away a child's human right to freedom of religion
   - can reinforce and continue religious prejudices which are harmful to society.

Now test yourself

1 Why might going to church make children believe in God?
2 Name two things Christian parents do to fulfil their promises at baptism.
3 Give one reason for thinking a religious upbringing is a good thing.
4 Give one reason for thinking a religious upbringing is a bad thing.

Answers on page 109

Topic 1.1.2 Religious experience

A religious experience is something which makes a person believe they have been in contact with God. This can take one of several forms:

● The **numinous** is a feeling of the presence of God such as when people are in a religious building, in a beautiful place or looking up at the stars on a clear night, and are filled with the awareness that there is something greater than them, which they feel to be God.

● **Conversion** is used to describe an experience of God, which is so great that the person experiencing it wants to change their life or religion and commit themselves to God in a special way.

● A **miracle** is an event that seems to break all the laws of science, and when people look for an explanation they can't find one and so they believe the only possible explanation is God.

● **Prayer** is a way for religious believers to make contact with God. If the person praying feels that God is listening to their prayer, then they are likely to believe that God exists.

Evaluation of religious experience

1 People who believe religious experience proves God exists may use these arguments:

  ● If you become aware of a presence greater than you in a numinous experience, you will think that God must exist.

  ● If you experience something that seems to break all the laws of science, the only explanation is God so he must exist.

  ● If a person prays and their prayer is answered (for example, when someone prays for a sick loved one to recover and they do) God must exist.

2 People who think it does not prove God exists may use these arguments:

  ● A numinous experience is caused by your surroundings, whether a church or the stars, and may have nothing to do with God.

  ● All miracles can be explained; for example, Jesus may not have been dead when he was taken down from the cross and so he just recovered rather than rising from the dead.

  ● There are more unanswered prayers than answered ones, so unanswered prayers surely prove God does not exist.

Key terms

Numinous – the feeling of the presence of something greater than you.

Conversion – when your life is changed by giving yourself to God.

Miracle – something which seems to break a law of science and makes you think only God could have done it.

Prayer – an attempt to contact God, usually through words.

Common mistake

Students often write about going to church/baptisms/weddings/funerals as a religious experience. You only get marks for this if you show clearly how they involved contact with God.

Now test yourself

Tested

1 What is prayer?
2 What does numinous mean?
3 What is a miracle?
4 What is conversion?

Answers on page 109

Topic 1.1.3 The argument from design

Design means making a plan to produce something. For example, a car is made to the plan of the designer, and looking at any part of the car makes you think the car has been designed.

Many religious believers have looked at the world and seen that the way the universe works makes it look as if it has been designed. Some scientists also see evidence of design in the process of evolution where complex life forms develop from simple ones. From this they have developed the argument from design:

- Anything that has been designed needs a designer.
- There is plenty of evidence that the world has been designed (laws of science such as gravity and magnetism, DNA being a blueprint for life, etc.).
- If the world has been designed, the world must have a designer.
- The only possible designer of the universe would be God.
- Therefore the appearance of design in the world proves that God exists.

Evaluation of the argument from design

1 Many religious believers think the design argument proves God's existence because:

- there is plenty of evidence that the universe has been designed (for example, laws of science, DNA, evolution)
- if something has been designed, it must have a designer
- only God could design something as wonderful as the universe.

Therefore God must exist.

2 Non-believers think the argument from design does not prove God exists because:

- no designer would have created destructive things like volcanoes, earthquakes, etc.
- science can explain the appearance of design without needing God
- the argument does not explain how such creations as dinosaurs could have been part of a design plan for the world
- even if the argument worked, it would only prove that the universe has a designer, not that the God of a particular religion exists.

Exam tip

Students often do not give enough reasons in part d) questions. You need to give three reasons for your opinion and three reasons for why some people may disagree with you.

Now test yourself

Tested

1 What have many religious believers and scientists developed from looking at the way the universe works?
2 Give two examples a religious believer might use as evidence that the universe has been designed.
3 What do non-believers claim can explain why the universe appears to be designed?
4 What do non-believers think would never have been created by a good designer?

Answers on page 109

Topic 1.1.4 The argument from causation

Causation is the process of one thing causing another. For example, a driver pressing the brake pedal causes the effect of the car slowing down.

Religious people use causation to prove God's existence in this way:

● Cause and effect seem to be a basic feature of the world. Whatever we do has an effect. If I do my homework (cause), I will please my parents and/or teachers (effect). Modern science has developed through looking at causes and effects, and scientific investigations seem to show that any effect has a cause and any cause has an effect.

● This means that the universe, the world and humans must have had a cause.

● God is the only logical cause of the universe.

● Therefore God must exist.

Evaluation of the argument from causation

1 Many religious people think the argument from causation proves God's existence because:

● the argument makes sense of ourselves and the universe because it explains how and why we are here

● the argument fits in with our common sense; we cannot believe that something can come from nothing and the argument shows that everything came from God

● the argument fits in with science, which tells us that every effect has a cause and so the universe (an effect) must have a cause (God)

● we believe that things must have started off – they must have a beginning – and the argument explains that God started off the universe and therefore is the First Cause.

2 Many non-religious people think the argument from causation does not prove God's existence because:

● if everything needs a cause then God must need a cause – why should the process stop with God?

● it is possible that matter itself is eternal and so was never created; that would mean that the process of causes could go back forever

● just because everything in the universe needs an explanation does not mean the universe needs an explanation; the universe could just have been there forever

● even if there was a First Cause it would not have to be the God of any particular religion; it could be good, evil, a mixture of good and evil, several gods, etc.

Exam tip
Make sure that you explain why some people disagree with the causation argument when answering an evaluation question.

Now test yourself

1 What is causation?
2 What does science teach about causation?
3 Who do believers think is the First Cause of the universe?
4 What do non-believers think the causation argument means that God would need?

Answers on page 109

Topic 1.1.5 Scientific explanations of the world

Science explains how the world came into being in this way:

- Matter is eternal.
- About 15 billion years ago, the matter of the universe exploded in a Big Bang.
- As the matter of the universe flew away from the explosion it formed stars and solar systems (the Red Shift Effect is evidence for this).
- The gases on the earth's surface produced primitive life whose genetic structure led to the evolution of new life forms and eventually humans.

How Christians respond to scientific explanations

1 Many Christians believe that the scientific explanations are true. However, they believe only God could have made the Big Bang at exactly the right microsecond to form the universe, and that God made the laws of science needed to form solar systems and life on earth. Therefore science needs God.

2 Some Christians believe that all the evidence for the Big Bang and evolution can be explained by Noah's Flood and Apparent Age theory, so the Bible is right.

3 Some Christians believe that both the scientific explanations and the Bible are correct, because the main points of the Bible story fit with science, but one of God's days in the creation story could be billions of years.

Evaluation of scientific explanations of the world

1 Some people think the scientific explanation proves that God does not exist because:

- if God existed, he would be the only explanation of the world but science can explain the world and humans without God
- there is no evidence that the Big Bang was caused by God
- an **omnipotent** and **omniscient** God would not have created the world in such a wasteful, evil way.

2 Some Christians believe the scientific explanation does not disprove God because:

- only God could have made the Big Bang at exactly the right microsecond to form the universe
- only God could have made the laws of science needed to form solar systems.

3 Other Christians believe the scientific explanation does not disprove God because:

- they believe the Bible account of creation is true
- they believe both the Bible and science could be correct.

Key terms

Omnipotent – the belief that God is all-powerful.

Omniscient – the belief that God knows everything that has happened and everything that is going to happen.

Exam tip

Read the questions carefully and try to relate them to what you know. For example, 'Explain why some scientists think creation does not need God' simply means 'What is the scientific explanation of the world?'

Now test yourself

1 When did the Big Bang happen?
2 What proves the universe is still expanding?
3 What was needed to form solar systems and life on earth?
4 What do some Christians believe can be explained by Noah's Flood and Apparent Age?

Answers on page 109

Topic 1.1.6 Unanswered prayers and belief in God

Unanswered prayers can lead a person to become an agnostic or an atheist because of the following reasons:

● If people say their prayers in church and at home, but never feel the presence of God when they pray, they may feel there is no God listening to them. The feeling that no one is listening to their prayers leads them to **agnosticism**, or even **atheism**.

● If someone prays for something good to happen, like a child to be cured of cancer or for the end of human suffering in wars, droughts, etc, and their prayers are not answered, then they may think God does not exist because if he did, he would not let such things happen.

How Christianity responds to unanswered prayers

Most Christians believe that God answers all prayers and that what seem to be unanswered prayers can be explained by the following:

● Selfish prayers are answered, but not in the way the person praying may want. For example, if you prayed for God to help you to pass an exam without any work, God will answer the prayer by not helping so that you work hard next time.

● Your prayer may not be answered in the way you expect because God has different plans; for example, he may want an ill person to enter heaven.

● Christians believe that God loves people and so they believe God's love will answer their prayers in the best possible way, even though it may not look like a direct answer.

● Christians have faith that God will answer all prayers in the best way for the person praying, or the people prayed for, even if it is different from what they expected.

Key terms

Agnosticism – not being sure whether God exists.

Atheism – believing that God does not exist.

Now test yourself

1 Feeling no one is listening to your prayers is likely to lead to what?
2 Praying for a child to be cured of a disease and them dying would be an example of what?
3 How might God answer a selfish prayer?
4 How do Christians believe God can answer all prayers?

Answers on page 109

Topic 1.1.7 Evaluation of unanswered prayers

1 People who believe unanswered prayers prove that God does not exist are likely to use such arguments as:

- Christians believe that God is their loving heavenly Father who will answer their prayers, so if he does not answer them, he can't exist.

- Christians are told about answered prayers – for example, people being cured of terminal cancer by prayer – but far more people have their prayers unanswered. A good God would not answer a few prayers for a cure and not answer lots of prayers for a cure. Therefore it is unlikely that God exists.

- If there was a God, he would answer the prayers of good religious people, and there would be no wars, no starvation, etc. The prayers of such people are clearly not answered, so God can't exist.

2 People who think unanswered prayers do not disprove God's existence are likely to use such arguments as:

- Your prayer may not be answered in the way you expect because God has different plans; for example, he may want an ill person to enter heaven.

- Just like a human parent, God may answer our prayers by giving us what we need rather than what we have asked for.

- Christians believe that God loves people and so they believe God's love will answer their prayers in the best possible way, even though it may not look like a direct answer.

> **Exam tip**
>
> When you are answering a b) question, make sure you say what your opinion is as well as giving two reasons for it.

Now test yourself

Tested

1 Why do Christians believe God will answer their prayers?
2 What do non-religious people believe would happen if God really answered prayers?
3 How could God answer prayers like a human parent?
4 What do Christians believe God's love will do?

Answers on page 109

Topic 1.1.8 Evil and suffering and belief in God

Evil and suffering can take two forms:

- **Moral evil** is caused by humans using their **free will**. Wars and crimes such as rape, murder and burglary are good examples of moral evil.

- **Natural evil** is suffering that has not been caused by humans. Earthquakes, floods, volcanoes, terminal illnesses and so on are not caused by humans, but they result in lots of human suffering.

Evil and suffering can cause people to question or reject belief in God because:

- if God is omnipotent (all-powerful), he must be able to remove evil and suffering from the world

- if God is **omni-benevolent** (all-good), he must want to remove evil and suffering from the world

- it follows that, if God exists, there should be no evil or suffering in the world

- as there is evil and suffering in the world, either God is not all-good and all-powerful or he does not exist.

Also, if God knows everything (omniscient), he must have known the evil and suffering that would come from creating the universe. So he should have created the universe in a way that avoided evil and suffering.

For many religious believers, evil and suffering become a problem if they experience it in their own lives when it can change them into an atheist or agnostic.

Key terms

Moral evil – actions done by humans which cause suffering.

Free will – the idea that human beings are free to make their own choices.

Natural evil – things which cause suffering but have nothing to do with humans.

Omni-benevolent – the belief that God is all-good.

Exam tip

If you are not sure what a key term means, don't use it.

Now test yourself

1 What name is given to the idea that human beings are free to make their own choices?
2 Give an example of moral evil.
3 Give an example of natural evil.
4 Why do evil and suffering make it difficult to believe God is both omnipotent and omni-benevolent?

Answers on page 109

Topic 1.1.9 Christian responses to evil and suffering

Christians believe evil and suffering do not disprove God's existence for the following reasons:

- The Bible shows that God must have a reason for allowing evil and suffering, but humans cannot understand it, so the correct response of Christians is to follow the example of Jesus and fight against evil and suffering.

- By making humans with free will, God created a world in which evil and suffering will come about through humans misusing their free will. So evil and suffering is a problem caused by humans, not God.

- The evil and suffering involved in this life are not a problem because this life is a preparation for paradise. If people are to improve their souls they need to face evil and suffering in order to become good, kind and loving. God cannot remove evil and suffering if he is going to give people the chance to become good people. But, in the end, he will show his omni-benevolence and omnipotence by rewarding the good in heaven.

- God has a reason for not using his power to remove evil and suffering, but humans cannot understand it. God is divine and there is no way humans can understand his thoughts.

Evaluation of Christian responses to evil and suffering

In evaluation questions, you will need to know these reasons why some people believe evil and suffering prove that God does not exist:

- If God is omnipotent, he must be able to remove evil and suffering from the world. If God is omni-benevolent, he must want to remove evil and suffering from the world. It follows that, if God exists, there should be no evil or suffering in the world. As there is evil and suffering in the world, God does not exist.

- A good God would not have designed a world with floods, earthquakes, volcanoes, terminal illness, etc. These cannot be blamed on humans and so they are evidence that God did not make the world and does not exist.

- An all-powerful God would not allow evil humans like Hitler and Stalin to cause so much suffering; so as individual humans have caused lots of suffering, God cannot exist.

- God is supposed to be omniscient, so he would have known the evil and suffering that would come from creating this universe. Therefore he should have created a different universe, and, as he did not, he can't exist.

Now test yourself

1. What do Christians believe the Bible tells them about God and evil and suffering?
2. What do some Christians believe is misused by people to create evil and suffering?
3. What do some Christians think this life is a preparation for?
4. How do some Christians believe God will eventually show his omni-benevolence and omnipotence?

Answers on page 109

Topic 1.1.10 Two programmes about religion and belief in God

Revised

You have to study in depth two programmes/films about religion and work out how they could affect a person's attitude to belief in God.

From your class notes you should have:

● a summary of each programme

● four pieces of evidence from each programme to show how it might have encouraged some people to believe in God

● four pieces of evidence from each programme to show how it might have encouraged some people not to believe in God

● what effect the programme had on your own attitude to belief in God and four reasons for this.

Evaluation of programmes about religion

You may be asked to argue for and against programmes/films about religion affecting belief in God.

1 To show that programmes/films do affect beliefs about God, you should:

> **either**

● use four pieces of evidence from a programme to show how it might have encouraged some people to believe in God

> **or**

● give four reasons why the programme affected your own attitude to belief in God.

2 To show how programmes/films do not affect beliefs about God, you should:

> **either**

● use four pieces of evidence from a programme to show how it would not have affected beliefs in God

> **or**

● give four reasons for why the programme did not affect your own attitude to belief in God.

> **Exam tip**
>
> Make sure that you identify the film or TV programme you are writing about.

> **Common mistake**
>
> Students often simply describe the film/programme. You only receive marks for explaining how it affects belief in God.

> **Now test yourself**
>
> Tested
>
> 1 Do you need to make a summary of the programmes you have seen?
> 2 How many pieces of evidence from each programme do you need to show how it might have encouraged some people to believe in God?
> 3 How many pieces of evidence from each programme do you need to show how it might have encouraged some people not to believe in God?
> 4 Do you need to work out what effect the programme had on your own beliefs about God?
>
> **Answers on page 109**

Exam practice

Answer both questions

1 a) What is natural evil? (2 marks)

  b) Do you think scientific explanations of the world show that God does not exist? Give two reasons for your point of view. (4 marks)

  c) Explain why the design argument leads some people to believe in God. (8 marks)

  d) 'Answered prayers prove that God exists.'

   (i) Do you agree? Give reasons for your opinion. (3 marks)

   (ii) Give reasons why some people may disagree with you. (3 marks)

   In your answer you should refer to at least one religion.

(Total: 20 marks)

2 a) What is free will? (2 marks)

  b) Do you think that programmes/films about religion can affect a person's beliefs about God? Give two reasons for your point of view. (4 marks)

  c) Explain why religious experience may lead some people to believe in God. (8 marks)

  d) 'There is no evidence that God exists.'

   (i) Do you agree? Give reasons for your opinion. (3 marks)

   (ii) Give reasons why some people may disagree with you. (3 marks)

   In your answer you should refer to at least one religion.

(Total: 20 marks)

Summary

- Having a religious upbringing is likely to lead to belief in God because children who have a religious upbringing are taught that God exists and spend most of their time with people who believe that God exists.

- Religious experience is when people feel God's presence. People claim to experience God in miracles, answered prayers, the numinous and conversion. Religious experience makes people feel that God is real, and so they believe he must exist.

- The design argument claims that the universe seems to be designed and, because anything that is designed must have a designer, God must exist because only God could have designed the universe.

- The argument from causation claims that the way everything seems to have a cause means the universe must have a cause. The only possible cause of the universe is God, so God must exist.

- Science says that matter is eternal and that the universe began when matter exploded and expanded, leading to the solar system. Life then developed on earth through evolution. Some people claim this means there is no God.

- Many Christians accept the scientific explanations but believe the Big Bang and evolution needed God in order to happen. Some Christians say the scientific explanations are wrong and the biblical story of creation is fact because it is the word of God. Some Christians believe that both science and the Bible are true because one of God's days in the creation story could be billions of years.

- If people do not feel God's presence when they pray, or if people pray for good things but their prayers are not answered, they may start to doubt God's existence.

- Christians believe that God cannot answer selfish prayers. But he answers all other prayers, though not always in the way people expect.

- Some people do not believe in God because they think that there would be no evil and suffering in a world created by a good and powerful God. A good God should not want such things to happen, and a powerful God ought to be able to get rid of them but does not.

- Christians respond to the problem of evil and suffering by: praying for those who suffer; helping those who suffer; claiming that evil and suffering are the fault of humans misusing their free will, or that they are part of a test to prepare people for heaven.

- You need to study two programmes/films about religion, and consider whether they encourage some people to believe in God or some people not to believe in God. You also need to consider whether they affected your beliefs about God.

Section 2 Matters of life and death

Topic 1.2.1 Christian beliefs about life after death

Revised

Why Christians believe in life after death

- The main Christian belief is that Jesus rose from the dead, as this is what is recorded in the Gospels and New Testament. This proves there is life after death.

- St Paul teaches in 1 Corinthians that people will have a **resurrection** like that of Jesus.

- The major creeds of the Church teach that Jesus rose from the dead and that there will be life after death. Christians should believe the creeds and so they should believe in life after death.

- Many Christians believe in life after death because it gives their lives meaning and purpose. They feel that a life after death where the good are rewarded and the evil punished makes sense of this life.

How beliefs about life after death affect the lives of Christians

- Christian beliefs about life after death mean Christians will try to live a good Christian life following the teachings of the Bible and the Church in order to go to heaven when they die.

- Living a good Christian life means loving God and loving your neighbour as yourself. So, Christians' lives will be affected as they try to love God by praying every day and by worshipping God every Sunday.

- The parable of the Sheep and Goats says those who do not help the poor will go to hell, encouraging Christians to help charities such as Christian Aid, CAFOD, etc.

- Christians believe that sin can prevent people from going to heaven, meaning that Christians will try to avoid committing sins in their lives so that they will go to heaven.

Evaluation of Christian beliefs about life after death

1 People who think Christians are right to believe in life after death would use the bullet points from 'Why Christians believe in life after death' to the left.

2 People who think they are wrong would use the arguments from Topic 1.2.4, page 16.

3 People who think beliefs about life after death make a difference to Christians' lives would use the bullet points to the left on how these beliefs affect Christians' lives.

4 People who think they make little difference would use facts such as:

- Christians have the same amount of divorce, children in care, etc, as non-Christians

- Christians do not give more to charity than non-Christians

- there are just as many Christians in prison as non-Christians.

Now test yourself
Tested

1 What belief about Jesus makes Christians believe in life after death?
2 Why do the creeds make Christians believe in life after death?
3 Why does the parable of the Sheep and Goats affect Christians' lives?
4 Why do Christians not want to die with unforgiven sins?

Answers on page 109

Key term

Resurrection – the belief that, after death, the body stays in the grave until the end of the world when it is raised.

Topic 1.2.2 Islam and life after death

If you have studied either Judaism, or Hinduism or Sikhism at school, you can find the revision notes for these on the website:
www.therevisionbutton.co.uk/myrevisionnotes

Why Muslims believe in life after death

● The Qur'an teaches that there is life after death. Muslims believe that the Qur'an is the word of God and so its teachings must be true.

● Muhammad taught that there is life after death. Muslims believe that the Prophet Muhammad is the last prophet and the perfect example for Muslims so his teachings must be true.

● Belief in life after death is one of the six fundamental beliefs of Islam which all Muslims are expected to believe. So Muslims must believe in life after death.

● Muslims believe that this life is a test from God which must involve a judgement as to how they have done in the test, and rewards for those who pass. This can only happen if there is life after death.

How beliefs about life after death affect the lives of Muslims

● Islam teaches that on the Last Day, all humans will be judged by God. Those who have lived good Muslim lives will go to paradise, and everyone else will go to hell. This affects Muslims' lives because they must try to live good Muslim lives to avoid hell.

● Living a good Muslim life means keeping the Five Pillars of Islam (declaring faith, praying five times a day, fasting during Ramadan, paying zakah, going on hajj). So their beliefs about life after death will have a big effect on their lives.

● Living a good Muslim life also means eating halal food, observing Muslim dress laws, not drinking alcohol, not gambling, nor being involved in lending at interest or receiving interest, etc.

● Muslim belief in resurrection means that nothing should be removed from the body after death. This affects Muslim lives because they try to avoid post-mortems and many Muslims have concerns about transplant surgery.

Evaluation of Islam and life after death

Evaluation questions will ask you to refer to only one religion, so you would be best just to use Christianity in answering evaluation questions, although you could use extra reasons from Islam.

> **Exam tip**
>
> If a question begins 'Choose one religion other than Christianity', make sure you begin your answer, 'I am going to write about Islam …'.

Now test yourself

1 Why do Muslims believe what the Qur'an says?
2 Why does the belief that life is a test make Muslims believe in life after death?
3 How does belief in the Last Day affect Muslims' lives?
4 What is involved in living a good Muslim life?

Answers on page 109

Topic 1.2.3 Non-religious reasons for believing in life after death

There are three main parts of the **paranormal** that provide non-religious reasons for believing in life after death.

1   **Near-death experiences:** About 8 per cent of people who are clinically dead for a time and then come back to life have a **near-death experience**. The main features of these experiences are: feelings of peace; floating above the body; seeing a bright light; entering a heavenly place where they see dead relatives. If near-death experiences are real, there must be life after death.

2   **Evidence for a spirit world:** Many people think of ghosts and ouija boards as evidence for a spirit world, but the clearest evidence comes from mediums. A medium is a person who claims to be able to communicate between our material world and a spirit world where the spirits of the dead live. There are mediums in all countries and in all religions. Mediums contact the dead and give information to living friends and relatives that there would be no way of them knowing had they not truly spoken to the dead. If mediums can contact the dead, there must be life after death.

3   **The evidence of reincarnation:** Some people believe in **reincarnation** and some religions have collected much evidence for this. If souls really are reborn in another body, then there is life after death.

Evaluation of non-religious reasons for believing in life after death

You may be asked to argue for and against the non-religious reasons for believing in life after death.

1   To argue for, you should use the reasons above.

2   To argue against, you could use these reasons:

- Near-death experiences have been challenged by most scientists, who claim they are simply products of the patient's brain as a result of chemical changes. Therefore there is no life after death.

- The evidence from mediums is also very suspect. Many mediums have been proven to be frauds. The only fool-proof test for mediums really contacting the spirit world (set by Robert Thouless) has never been passed by a medium. So they do not prove there is life after death.

- Most believers in life after death think that the mind or soul can survive without the body, but science shows that the mind cannot live without the brain, so when the body dies, the mind must also die.

> **Key terms**
>
> **Paranormal** – unexplained things which are thought to have spiritual causes, e.g. ghosts, mediums.
>
> **Near-death experience** – when someone about to die has an out-of-body experience.
>
> **Reincarnation** – the belief that, after death, souls are reborn in a new body.

> **Exam tip**
>
> To make sure you get top marks, use some key terms and specialist vocabulary in your answers to c) questions even if they come from a different section.

> **Now test yourself**
>
> 1   What is a near-death experience?
> 2   What do mediums claim to be able to do?
> 3   What do scientists claim about near-death experiences?
> 4   What does science show about the soul surviving death?
>
> **Answers on page 109**

Topic 1.2.4 Why some people do not believe in life after death

Revised

Some people do not believe in life after death because:

- they do not believe in God and if there is no God, there is no spirit world in which life after death can happen

- the different religions contradict each other about life after death, with Christianity, Islam and Judaism saying it will be resurrection or **immortality of the soul**, Hinduism, Sikhism and Buddhism saying it will be reincarnation; if life after death were true, they would all say the same thing

- much of the evidence is based on holy books, but they contradict each other, and there is no way of deciding which holy books are true and which false

- the evidence of the paranormal (near-death experiences, mediums, reincarnation) has all been challenged by scientists

- most believers in life after death think that the mind or soul can survive without the body, but science shows that the mind cannot live without the brain, so when the body dies, the mind must also die

- there is no place where life after death could take place; space journeys have shown heaven is not above the sky.

Key term

Immortality of the soul – the idea that the soul lives on after the death of the body.

Evaluation of why some people do not believe in life after death

You may be asked to argue for and against there being life after death.

1 If the question says 'in your answer, you should refer to at least one religion' to argue for there being life after death, you should use the reasons why Christians believe in life after death.

2 If the question does not ask you to refer to religion, you could use non-religious reasons.

3 To argue against there being life after death you should use the reasons above.

Exam tip

Always use the word 'atheist' rather than saying, 'people who do not believe in God'.

Now test yourself

Tested

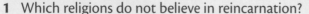

1 Which religions do not believe in reincarnation?

2 Give two examples of the paranormal.

3 What is the problem with using evidence from holy books?

4 What has science shown about the mind?

Answers on page 110

Topic 1.2.5 The nature of abortion

Revised

The law and abortion

The law says that **abortion** is only allowed if two doctors agree:

● the mother's life is at risk

● the mother's physical or mental health is at risk

● the child is very likely to be born severely handicapped

● there would be a serious effect on other children in the family.

Abortions cannot be carried out after 24 weeks of pregnancy, unless the mother's life is at risk or the foetus has severe disabilities.

Why abortion is a controversial issue

Abortion is a controversial issue because:

● many people believe that life begins at the moment of conception; therefore abortion is taking a human life

● many people believe that life begins when the foetus is able to live outside the mother; therefore abortion is not taking life

● many non-religious people believe that a woman should have the right to do what she wants with her own body; they might argue that an unwanted foetus is no different from an unwanted tumour

● many religious people believe that the unborn child's right to life is greater than the mother's rights

● some people argue the time limit should be reduced to eighteen or twenty weeks because of medical advances allowing foetuses to survive outside the womb

● there are also arguments about whether medical staff should have to carry out abortions.

Evaluation of the nature of abortion

You are not likely to be asked evaluation questions on this topic, but you are likely to be asked a b) question such as 'Do you think the law on abortion needs to be changed?'

1 If you think abortion should be banned, you can use religious arguments against abortion.

2 If you think the time limit should be reduced, you can argue that medical advances mean that foetuses can now be viable lives at 23 weeks and that it is wrong to take a viable life.

3 If you think the law should be changed to allow abortion on demand you could argue that life does not begin until the foetus can survive outside the mother and that a woman should have the right to do what she wants with her own body.

> **Key term**
>
> **Abortion** – the removal of a foetus from the womb before it can survive.

> **Common mistake**
>
> Students are often unaware that abortion on demand is not legal in the UK.

Now test yourself

Tested

1 Who has to agree to an abortion?

2 What is the time limit for abortions unless there is a risk to life?

3 When does life begin according to those who think abortion is murder?

4 When does life begin according to those who believe abortion should be allowed?

Answers on page 110

Topic 1.2.6 Christians and abortion

Revised

Christians have two differing attitudes to abortion:

1 The Catholic Church and Evangelical Protestant Churches teach that all abortion (apart from medical treatments for the mother which affect the life of the foetus) is wrong whatever the circumstances, because they believe that:

   - life belongs to God, so only God has the right to end a pregnancy

   - life begins at conception so abortion is taking life and this is banned in the Ten Commandments

   - they should follow the teaching of the Catholic Catechism (and Evangelical Protestant Churches) that all abortion is murder

   - counselling, help and adoption are alternatives to abortion for women made pregnant as a result of rape so that good can come out of evil in a new life.

2 Other Christians (mainly Liberal Protestants) disagree with abortion, but think it must be allowed in certain circumstances because they believe that:

   - life does not begin at conception

   - Jesus' command to love your neighbour means it is the duty of Christians to remove suffering, which abortion does

   - the **sanctity of life** can be broken in such things as a just war, so why not in a just abortion?

   - if doctors have developed tests for certain medical conditions in unborn babies, parents should be allowed abortions if such tests show their baby would be born with serious medical problems.

Evaluation of Christians and abortion

You are likely to be asked one of two types of evaluation question about abortion:

1 One type will say something like: 'No Christian/ religious person should ever have an abortion.' To answer this type of question you would use the reasons why some Christians think abortion is always wrong (part 1 to the left) to argue for; and the reasons why some Christians allow abortion (part 2 to the left) to argue against.

2 The other type will say something like: 'Every woman should have the right to an abortion if she wants one.' People who agree with this would use such reasons as:

   - life does not begin at conception; it begins when the foetus is capable of surviving outside the womb on its own, so abortion is not the same as murder

   - abortion prevents a great deal of suffering; if babies are brought into the world by mothers who do not want them and cannot afford to bring them up, the babies will suffer, the mothers will suffer, and society will suffer in dealing with the situation

   - a woman should have the right to do what she wants with her own body; they might argue that an unwanted foetus is no different from an unwanted tumour.

To argue against you should use the Christian reasons against abortion from part 1 at the top left of this page.

> **Key term**
>
> **Sanctity of life** – the belief that life is holy and belongs to God.

> **Now test yourself**
>
> Tested
>
> 1 Which Christians believe life does not begin at conception?
> 2 What does sanctity of life mean?
> 3 What does the Catholic Catechism teach about abortion?
> 4 Which of Jesus' commands is used by Christians to allow abortion?
>
> **Answers on page 110**

> **Common mistake**
>
> Some students forget that it is not just Catholic Christians who are against abortion; Evangelical Protestant Christians also oppose it.

Topic 1.2.7 Muslims and abortion

If you have studied either Judaism, or Hinduism or Sikhism at school, you can find the revision notes for these on the website: **www.therevisionbutton.co.uk/myrevisionnotes**

There are different attitudes to abortion among Muslims.

1 Many Muslims allow abortions up to 120 days of pregnancy for reasons such as the health of the mother or problems with the baby's health. The effect of having the baby on the present family can also be taken into consideration up to 120 days. They have this attitude because:

- some hadith say a foetus does not receive its soul until 120 days of pregnancy
- the Shari'ah says that the mother's life must always take priority.

2 Some Muslims believe that abortion should never be allowed. They believe this because:

- they believe life begins at the moment of conception
- the Qur'an says murder is wrong and they think abortion is murder.

3 Some Muslims believe that abortion can be allowed only if the mother's life is at risk. They believe this because:

- they believe the Qur'an bans abortion
- the death of the unborn child is a lesser evil than the death of the mother and the Shari'ah says that the mother's life must always take priority.

Evaluation of Muslims and abortion

Evaluation questions will ask you to refer to only one religion, so you would be best just to use Christianity in answering evaluation questions, although you could use extra reasons from Islam.

> **Common mistake**
>
> Students often say all Muslims are against abortion, which can lose you a lot of marks. Remember that Muslims have different views about abortion.

> **Now test yourself** — Tested
>
> 1 When does a foetus receive a soul according to the hadith?
> 2 Whose life must always take priority in Islam?
> 3 Why do some Muslims believe the Qur'an bans abortion?
> 4 What are the three attitudes to abortion in Islam?
>
> **Answers on page 110**

Topic 1.2.8 The nature of euthanasia

Euthanasia is normally thought of as providing a gentle and easy death to someone suffering from a painful, deadly disease and who has little **quality of life**. This can be done by:

- **assisted suicide**
- **voluntary euthanasia**
- **non-voluntary euthanasia**.

British law says that all these methods of euthanasia are murder. However, the law now agrees that stopping artificial feeding or not giving treatment (often called passive euthanasia) are not euthanasia and so are lawful.

Why euthanasia is a controversial issue

1 Many people want euthanasia to remain illegal because:

- there is always likely to be doubt as to whether it is what the person really wants
- there is also the problem as to whether the disease will end the life; a cure might be found for the disease
- it is the job of doctors to save lives, not end them; would patients trust doctors who kill their patients?
- people might change their mind, but then it would be too late
- who would check that it was only people who really wanted and needed euthanasia who died?

2 Many people want euthanasia to be made legal because:

- discoveries in medicine mean that people who would have died are being kept alive, often in agony, and they should have the right to die
- doctors have the right to switch off life-support machines if they think the patient has no chance of recovering, and allow people who have been in a coma for years to die; so euthanasia in this way is already legal
- people have a right to commit suicide, so why not give them the right to ask doctors to assist their suicide if they are too weak to do it alone?
- just as doctors can now switch off life-support machines, so judges have said that doctors can stop treatment.

Evaluation of the nature of euthanasia

You may be asked to argue for and against the law on euthanasia being changed (this means euthanasia becoming legal).

1 The arguments for euthanasia becoming legal would come from part 2 above.

2 The arguments against would come from part 1 above.

Key terms

Euthanasia – the painless killing of someone dying from a painful disease.

Quality of life – the idea that life must have some benefits for it to be worth living.

Assisted suicide – when a seriously ill person is provided with the means to commit suicide.

Voluntary euthanasia – ending life painlessly when someone in great pain asks for death.

Non-voluntary euthanasia – ending someone's life painlessly when they are unable to ask, but you have good reason for thinking they would want you to do so.

Now test yourself

1 What is euthanasia?
2 What is passive euthanasia?
3 What does British law say about euthanasia?
4 Why do discoveries in medicine make some believe the law on euthanasia should be changed?

Answers on page 110

Topic 1.2.9 Christians and euthanasia

Although all Christians believe that euthanasia is wrong, there are slightly different attitudes:

1 Catholics and many Liberal Protestants believe that assisted suicide, voluntary euthanasia and non-voluntary euthanasia are all wrong. However, they believe that switching off life-support machines, not giving treatment that could cause distress, and giving dying people painkillers are not euthanasia. They have this attitude because:

- they believe in the sanctity of life; life is created by God and so it is up to God, not humans, when people die

- they regard euthanasia as murder, which is forbidden in the Ten Commandments

- if doctors say someone is brain-dead, then they have already died, so switching off the machine is accepting what God has already decided

- if you give painkillers to a dying person in great pain, and they kill the person, this is not murder because your intention was to remove their pain, not to kill them (doctrine of double effect).

2 Some Christians believe any form of euthanasia is wrong, including switching off life-support machines, the refusal of extraordinary treatment, or the giving of large doses of painkillers. They have this attitude because:

- they take the Bible teachings literally and the Bible forbids suicide

- euthanasia includes switching off life-support machines, the refusal of extraordinary treatment, and giving large doses of painkillers because life is being ended by humans not God

- all forms of euthanasia are murder, which is banned by the Ten Commandments

- they believe that life is sacred and should only be taken by God; the Bible says that life and death decisions belong to God alone.

3 A few Christians accept euthanasia in certain circumstances because:

- medical advances mean it is hard to know what God's wishes about someone's death are; God may want someone to die but doctors are keeping them alive

- the teaching of Jesus on loving your neighbour can be used to justify assisting suicide, because it might be the most loving thing to do

- it is a basic human right to have control over your body and what people do to it; people have a right to refuse medical treatment, so why not a right to ask for euthanasia?

Evaluation of Christians and euthanasia

You may be asked to argue for and against euthanasia referring to at least one religion.

1 The arguments for euthanasia should come from part 2 of Topic 1.2.8 (page 20).

2 The argument against could be that Christians are against euthanasia because:

- the Bible bans suicide, and voluntary euthanasia is a form of suicide

- all forms of euthanasia are murder, which is forbidden by the Ten Commandments

- life is sacred and should only be taken by God; the Bible says that life and death decisions belong to God alone.

Now test yourself

1 Which Christians think that switching off life-support machines, not giving treatment that could cause distress, and giving dying people painkillers are not euthanasia?

2 The idea that life is created by God and so it is up to God, not humans, when people die is known as what?

3 What does the Bible ban that makes some Christians believe it bans euthanasia?

4 What is the connection between the Ten Commandments and euthanasia?

Answers on page 110

Common mistake

Students often assume that Catholics are against any form of euthanasia, just as they are with abortion. But the Catholic attitude to euthanasia is just the same as that of most Christians (part 1 above).

Topic 1.2.10 Muslims and euthanasia

Revised

If you have studied either Judaism, or Hinduism or Sikhism at school, you can find the revision notes for these on the website:
www.therevisionbutton.co.uk/myrevisionnotes

All Muslims are against euthanasia, but there are two slightly different attitudes.

1 Most Muslims are against all forms of euthanasia because:

- the Qur'an bans suicide and so assisted suicide is wrong, and most Muslims believe that voluntary euthanasia is just the same as assisted suicide

- Muslims believe that euthanasia is making yourself equal with God as you are taking over God's control of life and death, and this could be the greatest sin of shirk

- Muslims believe that euthanasia is murder, which is banned by the Qur'an

- Muslims believe life is a test from God and if people use euthanasia they are cheating in the test by trying to speed it up.

2 Some Muslims agree that euthanasia is wrong, but think switching off life-support machines is not euthanasia because:

- some Muslim lawyers have agreed to life-support machines being switched off when there are no signs of life

- if someone is brain-dead, God has already taken their life.

Evaluation of Muslims and euthanasia

Evaluation questions will ask you to refer to only one religion, so you would be best just to use Christianity in answering evaluation questions, although you could use extra reasons from Islam.

> **Exam tip**
>
> When answering c) questions on Islam and euthanasia, make sure you give four religious Muslim reasons.

> **Now test yourself**
> Tested
>
> 1 What connection does the Qur'an have to assisted suicide?
> 2 Why is euthanasia regarded as a form of shirk?
> 3 What does the Qur'an say about murder?
> 4 What connection does the belief that life is a test have to Muslim attitudes to euthanasia?
>
> **Answers on page 110**

Topic 1.2.11 The media and matters of life and death

The media are all forms of communication, including newspapers, television, radio, films and the internet. Remember that the word is plural.

1 Arguments that the media should not be free to criticise what religions say about matters of life and death:

- Some people believe that criticising what religions say on matters of life and death is a way of stirring up religious hatred, which is banned by the Racial and Religious Hatred Act of 2007. For example, when the Catholic Church withdrew support for Amnesty International because Amnesty supported abortion for women who had been raped, the media showed the Catholic position in a bad light.

- Many religious believers believe the freedom of the media should be limited because of the offence criticism of religious attitudes can cause. For example, when a Danish newspaper published cartoons of the Prophet Muhammad in 2006, there were riots in some countries.

- Some religious believers believe that criticising what religious leaders say about matters of life and death is close to the crime of blasphemy. If the media criticise the Pope's teachings on a topic like abortion, they are condemning the Catholic Church.

- Some religious people feel that religious statements are based on what God says and so are beyond human criticism.

2 Arguments that the media should be free to criticise what religions say about matters of life and death:

- Freedom of expression is a basic human right which is needed for democracy to work. Before people vote they need to know what is going on in the world and in their own country. For this they need a free media, and if the media have freedom of expression, then they must be free to criticise religious attitudes to matters of life and death.

- If religious leaders make use of the media to make statements about matters of life and death (as they do on things like stem-cell research), they must be prepared for the media to criticise those statements.

- In a multi-faith society such as the UK, there must be freedom of religious belief and expression. This means that the media must have the right to question and even criticise not only religious beliefs, but also what religions say about life and death issues.

- Life and death issues are so important to everyone that people want to know what is the right view. This could not be established if religions were allowed to put forward views that no one could criticise.

Evaluation of the media and matters of life and death

You may be asked to argue for and against the media being free to criticise religious attitudes to matters of life and death.

1 You should use the arguments that the media should be free from part 2 above.

2 You should use the arguments that the media should not be free from part 1 to the left.

Common mistake

Students often forget that newspapers (the press) are part of the media.

Now test yourself

1 Why do some believers think the Racial and Religious Hatred Act should be used to stop the media criticising religious attitudes?
2 If people believe that what religious leaders say is what God says, what does that make media criticism of religious leaders?
3 How can human rights be used to defend media criticism of religious attitudes?
4 What type of society has to have freedom of expression on religion?

Answers on page 110

Exam practice

Answer both questions

1 **a)** What is quality of life? (2 marks)

b) Do you think there is life after death? Give two reasons for your point of view. (4 marks)

c) Explain how their beliefs about life after death affect the lives of Christians. (8 marks)

d) 'Religious people should never have abortions.'

(i) Do you agree? Give reasons for your opinion. (3 marks)

(ii) Give reasons why some people may disagree with you. (3 marks)

In your answer, you should refer to at least one religion.

(Total: 20 marks)

2 **a)** What is immortality of the soul? (2 marks)

b) Do you think the media should be free to criticise what religion says about matters of life and death? Give two reasons for your point of view. (4 marks)

c) Choose one religion other than Christianity and explain why its followers believe in life after death. (8 marks)

d) 'Everyone should have the right to euthanasia if they have no quality of life.'

(i) Do you agree? Give reasons for your opinion. (3 marks)

(ii) Give reasons why some people may disagree with you. (3 marks)

In your answer you should refer to at least one religion.

(Total: 20 marks)

Summary

- Christians believe in life after death because Jesus rose from the dead and the Bible and the creeds say there is life after death. The Church teaches that there is life after death and the soul is something that can never die. Their beliefs about life after death affect their lives because Christians will try to love God and love their neighbour so that they go to heaven and not hell.

- Muslims believe in life after death because it is taught in the Qur'an, in the hadith of the Prophet and is one of the essential six beliefs of Islam. Their beliefs about life after death affect their lives because Muslims will try to follow the Five Pillars and the teachings of the Shari'ah so that they go to heaven and not hell.

- Some people believe in life after death for non-religious reasons such as near-death experiences, evidence of the spirit world through ghosts, mediums, etc, and evidence of reincarnation such as people remembering previous lives.

- Some people do not believe in life after death because they do not believe in God. Other believe there is no scientific evidence or they do not see where life after death could take place.

- Abortion is allowed in the United Kingdom if two doctors agree that there is medical reason for it. Abortion is a controversial issue because people disagree about when life begins, whether abortion is murder and whether a woman has the right to choose. Catholics and Evangelical Protestants believe abortion is always wrong because it is murder and against God's will. Liberal Protestants allow abortion as the lesser of two evils.

- Some Muslims think abortion should never be allowed. Some Muslims think abortion can only be allowed if the mother's life is in danger. Some Muslims think abortion is allowed until 120 days because this is when the foetus receives its soul.

- There are various types of euthanasia which are all aimed at giving an easy death to those suffering intolerably. British law says that euthanasia is a crime, but withholding treatment to dying patients is not. Euthanasia is a controversial issue because medicine can keep people alive with little quality of life, suicide is no longer a crime, we give euthanasia to suffering animals and the role of doctors is to save life not take it away.

- All Christians are against euthanasia because they believe life is sacred and belongs to God. However, there are some different attitudes among Christians about switching off life-support machines, withdrawing treatment, etc, because most think these are not euthanasia.

- All Muslims are against euthanasia because they believe life is sacred and belongs to God. However, there are some different attitudes among Muslims about the switching off of life-support machines, withdrawing treatment, etc, because some think these are not euthanasia.

- Some people think that what religions say about matters of life and death should not be criticised by the media because they might stir up religious hatred and are offensive to religious believers. Other people think the media should be free to criticise religious attitudes because a free media is a key part of democracy and if religions want to be free to say what they want, then the media must be free to criticise religion.

Section 3 Marriage and the family

Topic 1.3.1 Changing attitudes to marriage and family life

Revised

In the UK in the 1960s, it was expected that young people only had sex after marriage. Most people married young, in church, and marriage was for life. Families were husband and wife and children (**nuclear family**) and male homosexuality was a criminal offence. However, attitudes have changed.

Cohabitation and marriage

Most people have sex before marriage and many couples live together (**cohabit**) rather than marry. The average age for marrying has increased and most marriages do not take place in church. This has happened because:

● effective **contraception** has made it safer to have sex before marriage

● fewer people go to church and so do not see a need to keep sex until after marriage

● the media, and celebrities cohabiting, make cohabitation look respectable and show sexual relationships outside of marriage as the norm.

Divorce

There are many more divorces, and divorce is now accepted as a normal part of life. This has happened because:

● new laws have made divorce much cheaper and easier for ordinary people

● increased equality for women means that women are no longer prepared to accept unequal treatment from men

● there has been a great change in how long people are likely to be married as life expectancies are much longer

● many women are now financially independent and can support themselves after a divorce.

Family life

There are:

● more families with unmarried parents because of the popularity of cohabitation

● more **reconstituted families** because of the increase in divorce and **re-marriage**

● more single-parent families because of the increase in divorce, and the acceptance of unmarried mothers also means there are more single-parent families

● more extended families because more mothers are in paid employment and use retired grandparents or close relatives to look after their children.

> ### Key terms
>
> **Nuclear family** – mother, father and children living as a unit.
>
> **Cohabitation** – living together without being married.
>
> **Contraception** – intentionally preventing pregnancy from occurring.
>
> **Reconstituted family** – where two sets of children (stepbrothers and stepsisters) become one family when their divorced parents marry each other.
>
> **Re-marriage** – marrying again after being divorced from a previous marriage.

Homosexuality

Society treats homosexual sex the same way as heterosexual sex, and homosexual couples can now form a legal union (**civil partnership**) that gives them the same rights and treatment as an opposite-sex married couple. This has happened because:

● changes in the laws have made it easier to be openly homosexual and made society more aware of homosexuality

● medical research has shown that **homosexuality** is natural, leading people to accept equal status and rights for homosexual couples

● media coverage of gay celebrities has led to a greater acceptance of all gay people, as has the work of gay-rights organisations.

Evaluation of changing attitudes to marriage and family life

Evaluation questions are likely to ask you to refer to at least one religion so the advice on evaluation questions is at the end of Topics 1.3.2, 1.3.4, 1.3.6 and 1.3.8.

Key terms

Civil partnership – a legal ceremony giving a homosexual couple the same legal rights as a husband and wife.

Homosexuality – sexual attraction to the same sex.

Now test yourself   Tested ☐

1 What is the word for living together without being married?
2 Why has divorce increased?
3 Why has the number of re-constituted families increased?
4 What benefits does a civil partnership give a gay couple?

Answers on page 110

Common mistake

When a question asks, 'Why have attitudes changed?' students often just describe how they have changed instead of giving reasons.

Topic 1.3.2 Christians and sex outside marriage

Most Christians believe sex outside marriage is wrong because:

- God gave us sex for the **procreation** of children who should be brought up in a Christian family, so sex should only take place within a marriage
- the Bible says that sex outside of marriage is sinful and Christians should follow the teachings of the Bible
- the Catechism says that **pre-marital sex** is wrong and likely to lead to **promiscuity**, and Catholics should follow the teachings of the Catechism
- all Christians are against **adultery** because it breaks the wedding vows
- adultery is also banned by the Ten Commandments, which all Christians should follow
- adultery is condemned by Jesus, and all Christians should follow the teachings of Jesus.

Some Christians accept that couples may live together before marriage, but only in a long-term relationship leading to marriage.

Evaluation of Christians and sex outside marriage

1 You are likely to be asked to argue for and against allowing sex before marriage.
People who agree with sex before marriage are likely to use such reasons as:

- sex is a natural result of two people being in love, and there is no reason for them to wait until they are married
- modern contraception means that a couple can have sex without the risk of pregnancy, so unwanted children are not likely to result from sex before marriage
- sex before marriage is now accepted by society and very few people think it is wrong.

For why Christians disagree with sex before marriage use the reasons at the top of the page.

2 You may also be asked to argue for and against getting married rather than living together. Christians believe marriage is better than living together because:

- marriage is God's gift (a sacrament for many Christians), and the way God says humans should have sex and bring up a family
- the Bible teaches that sex should only take place in marriage and that marriage is necessary for the upbringing of a Christian family
- the Church teaches that marriage is the basis of society and that living together without marriage is wrong
- statistics show that married couples are more likely to stay together than cohabiting couples and that the children of married couples have a more stable and happy life.

People who believe living together is as good as marriage give such reasons as:

- couples who live together can be just as happy and committed as those who marry
- you cannot promise to stay with someone until death if you do not know what it will be like to live with them
- living together brings all the commitment and joy of marriage without the legal complications
- weddings are expensive and living together allows a couple to spend that money on the home, children, etc.

Key terms

Procreation – making a new life.

Pre-marital sex – sex before marriage.

Promiscuity – having sex with a number of partners without commitment.

Adultery – a sexual act between a married person and someone other than their marriage partner.

Now test yourself

Tested

1 What does the Bible say about pre-marital sex?
2 Give two reasons why Christians are against adultery.
3 Why has modern contraception led to more pre-marital sex?
4 What shows that married couples are more likely to stay together than cohabiting couples?

Answers on page 110

Exam tip

When questions ask about sex outside marriage, that means you must answer on both pre-marital sex and adultery.

Topic 1.3.3 Muslims and sex outside marriage

Revised

If you have studied either Judaism, or Hinduism or Sikhism at school, you can find the revision notes for these on the website:
www.therevisionbutton.co.uk/myrevisionnotes

Muslims believe that sex outside of marriage is wrong because:

- sex before marriage is forbidden by the Qur'an, and Muslims believe the Qur'an is the word of God
- the Shari'ah says that sex should only take place in marriage
- Islam teaches that sex is for the procreation of children who should be raised in a family where the mother and father are married
- adultery is condemned by God in the Qur'an
- adultery breaks the marriage contract that both husband and wife have agreed to
- adultery is likely to harm the family, and harming the family is condemned by both the Qur'an and Shari'ah.

Evaluation of Muslims and sex outside marriage

Evaluation questions will ask you to refer to only one religion, so it would be best just to use Christianity in answering evaluation questions, although you could use extra reasons from Islam.

> **Exam tip**
>
> In any question on Muslim beliefs, you should always mention that Muslims believe something because the Qur'an says so and they believe the Qur'an is the direct word of God.

Now test yourself

Tested

1 Why do Muslims believe they should obey what the Qur'an says?
2 What does the Shari'ah say about sex?
3 What does adultery break?
4 Which Muslim authorities condemn harming the family?

Answers on page 110

Topic 1.3.4 Christians and divorce

There are two different attitudes to divorce in Christianity.

The Catholic Church

The Catholic Church does not allow religious divorce or re-marriage. The only way a marriage between baptised Catholics can be ended is by the death of one of the partners.

However, the Catholic Church does allow civil divorce if that will be better for the children, but the couple are still married in the eyes of God and so cannot re-marry. Catholics have this attitude because:

● Jesus taught that divorce is wrong and Christians should follow his teachings

● the couple have made a covenant with God which 'cannot be broken by any earthly power'

● the Catechism teaches that a marriage cannot be dissolved and so religious divorce is impossible

● there can be no re-marriage as there can be no religious divorce, so re-marriage would be both bigamy (having two husbands or wives) and adultery. (However, if it can be proved that the marriage was never a true Christian marriage, Catholics can have an annulment, which makes them free to re-marry.)

Non-Catholic Churches

Most non-Catholic Churches think that divorce is wrong, but allow it if the marriage has broken down and permit divorced people to re-marry. They are sometimes asked to promise that this time their marriage will be for life. Non-Catholic Churches allow divorce because:

● Jesus allowed divorce in the Bible in Matthew 19:9 for a partner's adultery

● if a marriage has really broken down then the effects of the couple not divorcing would be a greater evil than the evil of divorce itself ('the lesser of two evils')

● if Christians repent and confess their sins they can be forgiven; this means a couple should have another chance at marriage if they are keen to make it work this time

● these Churches believe it is better to divorce than to live in hatred and quarrel all the time.

Evaluation of Christians and divorce

For arguments in favour of divorce use the non-Catholic reasons for allowing divorce above. For arguments against divorce use the Catholic reasons for not allowing divorce at the top of the page.

> **Exam tip**
>
> When answering questions which ask why some Christians allow divorce and some do not, remember to give two religious reasons for the Catholic view and two religious reasons for the Protestant view.

Now test yourself

1 What is the only way marriage can be ended for Catholic Christians?
2 What does the Catechism say about divorce?
3 Why do non-Catholic Christians think that Matthew 19:9 allows divorce?
4 How do non-Catholic Christians use the idea of 'the lesser of two evils' to justify divorce?

Answers on page 110

Topic 1.3.5 Muslims and divorce

If you have studied either Judaism, or Hinduism or Sikhism at school, you can find the revision notes for these on the website:
www.therevisionbutton.co.uk/myrevisionnotes

Most Muslims believe that divorce should be allowed because:

- the Qur'an permits divorce and sets out the terms for custody of children and care for divorced wives

- the Shari'ah permits divorce and has many laws about how divorce and re-marriage should operate

- most Muslims believe divorce is a lesser evil than forcing a couple to live in hatred and bitterness

- marriage is a contract in Islam and the contract says what is to happen if the couple divorce, so divorce must be allowed.

Some Muslims would not divorce because:

- Muhammad is reported to have said that divorce is the most hated of lawful things and they follow what Muhammad said

- most marriages are arranged by families, so there is family pressure against divorce

- many Muslims believe they will be sent to hell if they harm their children, and divorce is likely to harm the children

- the Qur'an teaches that families should try to rescue the marriage before they divorce.

Common mistake

Students often say that Islam does not allow divorce. This loses marks because divorce is allowed in the Qur'an, and so most Muslims allow divorce.

Evaluation of Muslims and divorce

Evaluation questions will ask you to refer to only one religion, so it would be best just to use Christianity in answering evaluation questions, although you could use extra reasons from Islam.

Now test yourself

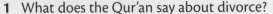

Tested

1 What does the Qur'an say about divorce?
2 What does the Shari'ah say about divorce?
3 What did Muhammad say about divorce?
4 Why is there family pressure against divorce in Islam?

Answers on page 110

Topic 1.3.6 Christians and the family

Family life is important for Christians because:

- one of the main purposes of Christian marriage is to have children and bring them up in a Christian environment so that they become good Christians

- Christianity teaches that the family was created by God as the basis of society and is the only place for the upbringing of children

- Christian teaching on divorce shows that the family is too important to be broken up by divorce

- without the family, children would not learn the difference between right and wrong

- the family is very important for Christianity to continue and grow as it is the family that brings children into the faith.

However, Jesus taught that there are more important things than the family, which is why Catholic priests, nuns and monks leave their families so that they can serve God.

Evaluation of Christians and the family

You may be asked to argue for and against family life being more important for religious than non-religious people.

1 You could use any of the main points above for family life being more important for Christians than non-religious people.

2 You could use the following arguments against family life being more important for religious than non-religious people:

  - many non-religious people see their family as being the most important thing in their lives, whereas many religious people see their religion as more important than their family

  - most non-religious people have just as good a family life as religious people

  - non-religious families may be able to respect their children more because they do not have a duty to force them to take part in religion

  - religion cannot make a difference to how much parents love their children, and children love their parents.

> **Exam tip**
>
> Use four religious reasons if you are asked to explain why the family is important for Christians.

Now test yourself

1 What is the purpose of Christian marriage connected with the family?
2 Why do Christians believe God created the family?
3 What do Catholic priests, nuns and monks do to their families?
4 Why might non-religious people be able to respect their children more than Christians?

Answers on page 110

Topic 1.3.7 Muslims and the family

Revised

If you have studied either Judaism, or Hinduism or Sikhism at school, you can find the revision notes for these on the website:
www.therevisionbutton.co.uk/myrevisionnotes

Family life is important in Islam because:

● Muslim parents will be judged by God on how well they have brought up their children; if family life decides whether Muslims go to heaven, it must be very important

● the Qur'an teaches that the family was created by God as the basic unit of society and as the only place in which children should be brought up

● the Prophet Muhammad married and raised a family, so Muslims must marry and raise a family

● without the family, children would not learn the difference between right and wrong

● the family is very important for Islam to continue and grow as it is the family that brings children into the faith.

Evaluation of Muslims and the family

Evaluation questions will ask you to refer to only one religion, so you would be best just to use Christianity in answering evaluation questions, although you could use extra reasons from Islam.

Common mistake

Students often mix up Christian and Muslim reasons for family life being important. If you are answering on Islam, make sure your reasons are clearly Muslim.

Now test yourself

Tested

1 For Muslims, how does family life relate to going to heaven?
2 What does the Qur'an teach about the family?
3 What example did the Prophet Muhammad set for family life?
4 What does the family do which is important for the future of Islam?

Answers on page 111

Topic 1.3.8 Christians and homosexuality

Catholic Christians

Catholic Christians believe that being a homosexual is not a sin but that homosexual sexual activity is a sin. The Catholic Church asks homosexuals to live without any sexual activity and believes they will be helped to do this by the sacraments of the Church. The Church believes that it is sinful to criticise homosexuals or attack their behaviour. Catholics have this attitude because:

● the Bible condemns homosexual activity

● it is the tradition of the Church that any sexual activity should have the possibility of creating children

● it is the teaching of the Magisterium which Catholics should believe

● the Church teaches that people cannot help their sexual orientation, but they can control their sexual activity

● discriminating against people because of their sexual orientation is similar to racism, which is sinful.

Evangelical Protestants

Evangelical Protestants believe that homosexuality is a sin and that homosexuals can be changed by the power of the Holy Spirit. The reasons for this attitude are:

● the Bible says that homosexuality is a sin and they believe that the Bible is the direct word of God

● they believe that the salvation of Christ can remove all sins, including homosexuality

● all the Churches have taught that homosexuality is wrong, even though some now say it is not.

Liberal Protestants

Many Liberal Protestants welcome homosexuals into the Church, and accept homosexual relationships. Some Liberal Protestants provide blessings for civil partnerships. The reasons for this attitude are:

● they believe that the Bible texts condemning homosexuality show beliefs at the time rather than being the word of God

● they feel that the major Christian belief in love and acceptance means that homosexuals must be accepted

● many believe that if homosexual Christians feel the Holy Spirit approves of their homosexuality, it must be true

● they believe that Christians should be open and honest and so gay Christians should not be made to tell lies and pretend to be heterosexual.

Evaluation of Christians and homosexuality

You may be asked to argue for and against giving equal rights to homosexuals (similar arguments could be used for questions on whether Christians or religious people can be homosexual).

1   Arguments for giving equal rights:

● British law gives equal rights to homosexuals, and equal rights are part of their basic human rights.

● Medical research has shown that homosexuality is probably genetic and therefore natural, so homosexuals should have equal status and rights.

● Many Liberal Protestants feel that the major Christian belief in love and acceptance means that homosexuals must be given equal rights.

2   For arguments against giving equal rights to homosexuals use the arguments of the Catholic Christians and Evangelical Protestants given to the left.

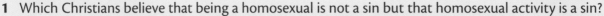

Now test yourself

1   Which Christians believe that being a homosexual is not a sin but that homosexual activity is a sin?

2   Which Christians believe that the Bible texts condemning homosexuality show beliefs at the time rather than being the word of God?

3   Which Christians believe that homosexuality is a sin and that homosexuals can be changed by the power of the Holy Spirit?

4   What has shown that homosexuality is probably genetic and therefore natural?

Answers on page 111

Topic 1.3.9 Muslims and homosexuality

Revised

If you have studied either Judaism, or Hinduism or Sikhism at school, you can find the revision notes for these on the website:
www.therevisionbutton.co.uk/myrevisionnotes

Most Muslims believe that homosexuality is wrong because:

- homosexuality is condemned by the Qur'an and the Qur'an is the final word of God
- the Prophet Muhammad condemned homosexuality in several hadith, and Muslims should follow his teachings
- God says in the Qur'an that marriage between a man and a woman is the only lawful form of sex
- Islam teaches that any sexual activity should have the possibility of creating children, which homosexual sex cannot
- all Muslims should try to have a family, but homosexuals cannot.

Some Muslims believe that homosexuality is acceptable because:

- they believe that Islam is a religion of tolerance, not hate
- they believe that God created and loves all people whatever their sexual orientation
- they believe that scientific evidence about homosexuality means that God must have made some people homosexual.

Evaluation of Muslims and homosexuality

You may be asked to argue for and against civil partnerships, but you will be asked to refer to only one religion so these arguments just use Christianity.

1 Arguments for civil partnerships:

- They allow homosexual couples to commit themselves to each other and encourage stable sexual relationships.
- They allow homosexual couples to share their belongings, pensions, etc, in just the same way as heterosexual couples.
- They are a way of encouraging the Christian virtues of love and **faithfulness** among homosexuals.

2 Arguments against civil partnerships:

- Christianity teaches that God gave marriage for a man and a woman, not two people of the same sex.
- One of the purposes of Christian marriage is for the procreation of children and, as homosexuals cannot procreate, they should not marry.
- Christians who believe homosexuals should not be sexually active cannot accept civil partnerships because they encourage homosexual sexual activity.

Key term

Faithfulness – staying with your marriage partner and having sex only with them.

Exam tip

When you refer to the Qur'an or hadith, always explain that Muslims should obey the Qur'an because it is the word of God and follow the hadith because they are the guidance of God's final prophet.

Now test yourself

Tested

1 What does the Qur'an say about homosexuality?
2 Who condemned homosexuality in several hadith?
3 What is the only lawful form of sex according to the Qur'an?
4 What makes some Muslims believe that God must have made some people homosexual?

Answers on page 111

Topic 1.3.10 Christians and contraception

The Catholic Church teaches that couples should use natural family planning rather than artificial methods of contraception because:

● Pope Paul VI stated that the only allowable forms of contraception are natural methods, and this teaching has been confirmed in the Catechism of the Catholic Church

● the Church teaches that all sex should be unitive (bringing the couple together) and creative (bringing new life)

● some contraceptives bring about a very early abortion (abortifacient) and Catholics believe abortion is wrong.

Almost all non-Catholic Christians believe that all forms of contraception are permissible because:

● Christianity is about love and justice, and contraception improves women's health and raises their standard of living, giving them society's love and justice

● God created sex for enjoyment and to strengthen marriage so there does not have to be the possibility of creation of children

● there is nothing in the Bible that forbids the use of contraception

● they believe that using condoms is the best way to combat HIV/AIDS.

Evaluation of Christians and contraception

For arguments for contraception use the non-Catholic reasons above for allowing contraception. For arguments against contraception use the Catholic reasons at the top of the page for not allowing contraception.

> **Exam tip**
>
> When questions ask you to explain why Christians have different attitudes to contraception, make sure to give at least two reasons why Catholic Christians are against all artificial methods of contraception and two reasons why other Christians allow them.

Now test yourself

1 Which Christians believe that the only allowable forms of contraception are natural methods?
2 Which Christians believe that all forms of contraception are permissible?
3 Which Church teaches that all sex should be both unitive and creative?
4 Which Christians believe that sex can be just unitive and does not have to be creative?

Answers on page 111

Topic 1.3.11 Muslims and contraception

If you have studied either Judaism, or Hinduism or Sikhism at school, you can find the revision notes for these on the website:
www.therevisionbutton.co.uk/myrevisionnotes

All Muslims believe that they should have children, but there are different attitudes as to whether contraception can be used to limit the number of children.

Some Muslims believe that contraception should not be used at all because:

● they believe the Qur'an's command, 'You should not kill your children for fear of want', means a ban on contraception

● they believe that God created sex for having children

● they are opposed to abortion and so would not allow any contraceptives that acted as abortifacients

● they believe it is the duty of Muslims to have large families.

Some Muslims believe that it is permitted for Muslims to use contraception to limit the number of children because:

● there are several hadith which record that the Prophet permitted the use of coitus interruptus as a means of contraception

● the Qur'an says God does not place extra burdens on his followers, and contraception stops extra burdens

● if pregnancy risks a mother's health, contraception must be allowed because Islam puts the mother's life first

● Muslim lawyers agree that contraception is different from abortion and so should be permitted.

Evaluation of Muslims and contraception

Evaluation questions will ask you to refer to only one religion, so it would be best just to use Christianity in answering evaluation questions, although you could use extra reasons from Islam.

Common mistake

Some students think that all Muslims are against contraception when most are not.

Now test yourself

Tested

1 What do some Muslims believe 'You should not kill your children for fear of want' means for contraception?
2 Why would some Muslims not use abortifacient contraceptives?
3 Why do Muslims believe contraception should be used if pregnancy threatens the mother's health?
4 Who agrees that contraception is different from abortion?

Answers on page 111

Exam practice

Answer both questions

1 a) What is faithfulness? (2 marks)

   b) Do you think Christians should have sex before marriage? Give two reasons for your point of view. (4 marks)

   c) Explain why some Christians allow divorce and re-marriage, but others do not. (8 marks)

   d) 'Religious people should not use contraceptives.'

   (i) Do you agree? Give reasons for your opinion. (3 marks)

   (ii) Give reasons why some people may disagree with you. (3 marks)

   In your answer you should refer to at least one religion.

   (Total: 20 marks)

2 a) What is procreation? (2 marks)

   b) Do you think religious people can be homosexual? Give two reasons for your point of view. (4 marks)

   c) Explain why attitudes to divorce and marriage have changed. (8 marks)

   d) 'Living together is just as good as being married.'

   (i) Do you agree? Give reasons for your opinion. (3 marks)

   (ii) Give reasons why some people may disagree with you. (3 marks)

   In your answer you should refer to at least one religion.

   (Total: 20 marks)

Summary

- Fifty years ago, most people only had sex in marriage, and they married in church. Today, people have sex before they marry, cohabitation is acceptable and most marriages are not in church. This is probably because of safer contraception and religion having less influence.

- Divorce and re-marriage were rare and disapproved of, but today divorce and re-marriage are accepted, and two in five marriages end in divorce. The changes may have been caused by cheaper divorce and women having more equality.

- Family life has changed as there are more one-parent families and re-constituted families, probably caused by the changing attitudes to sex, marriage and divorce.

- Homosexuality used to be illegal, but now homosexuals have the same rights to sexual activity as heterosexuals, including civil partnerships. This is probably due to discoveries showing that homosexuality is natural and to changes to the law.

- All Christians believe adultery is wrong as it breaks one of the Ten Commandments. Most Christians believe that sex before marriage is wrong because the Church and the Bible teach this.

- Muslims believe that sex before marriage and adultery are wrong because the Qur'an teaches this.

- Catholics do not allow religious divorce and re-marriage because they believe the marriage vows cannot be broken. Other Christians disapprove of divorce, but allow religious divorce and re-marriage if the marriage has broken down, because Christianity teaches forgiveness.

- Most Muslims allow divorce because it is permitted by the Qur'an. Some Muslims do not allow divorce because Muhammad said God disapproves of it.

- Christians believe that the family is important because it is taught in the Bible and Christian marriage services refer to bringing up a family as one of the main purposes of marriage. Christians believe that the family was created by God.

- Family life is important in Islam because the Qur'an says that the family is the basis of society and Muslims should follow the example of Muhammad, who raised a family.

- Catholics believe there is nothing wrong with homosexual feelings or relationships as long as there is no sexual activity, because this is the teaching of the Church. Evangelical Protestants believe that homosexuality is sinful because it is condemned in the Bible. Liberal Protestants believe that homosexuality is acceptable because it is natural, and Christians should love and accept everyone.

- Most Muslims believe that homosexuality is wrong because it is condemned in the Qur'an and Shari'ah. A few Muslims believe that homosexuality should be accepted because it was created by God and Islam is a religion of peace and tolerance.

- The Catholic Church teaches that using artificial methods of contraception to stop a baby being conceived is wrong. God gave sex in order to create children. Other Christians allow the use of contraception because they believe God gave sex to strengthen a marriage.

- Some Muslims are against the use of contraceptives because they believe God created sex for procreation. Other Muslims agree with contraception because the Prophet and law schools do.

Section 4 Religion and community cohesion

Topic 1.4.1 Changing attitudes to the roles of men and women in the UK

Revised

During the second half of the nineteenth century it became the accepted view that married women should stay at home and look after the children. However, attitudes have changed greatly and women can now:

- keep their property separate from that of their husband
- vote in elections
- become councillors and MPs
- receive the same pay as men for the same work (Equal Pay Act)
- not be discriminated against in employment on grounds of gender or marriage (Sex **Discrimination** Act).

The main causes for the changes were:

- the suffragette movement, which showed that women were no longer prepared to be treated as second-class citizens
- women successfully taking on men's jobs during the First and Second World Wars
- the development of equal rights for women in other countries, which made it difficult to claim they were not needed in the UK
- social and industrial developments in the 1950s and 1960s, which led to the need for more women workers
- the UN Declaration of Human Rights and the development of the feminist movement, which meant equal rights had to be accepted
- the Labour governments of 1964–70 and 1974–79, which were dedicated to equal rights for women.

However, social attitudes have been slower to change and **sexism** means women are still more likely to do the housework, and have fewer promotion prospects and lower salaries than men.

Evaluation of changing attitudes to the roles of men and women

Evaluation questions are likely to ask you to refer to at least one religion so the advice on evaluation questions comes in Topic 1.4.2, page 41.

> **Key terms**
>
> **Discrimination** – treating people less favourably because of their ethnicity/gender/colour/sexuality/age/class.
>
> **Sexism** – discriminating against people because of their gender (being male or female).

> **Exam tip**
>
> Questions asking why attitudes have changed require you to give four reasons for the changes. Questions asking how attitudes have changed require you to describe four ways in which they have changed.

> **Now test yourself** ───────────────── Tested
>
> 1 What right did the Equal Pay Act give women?
> 2 What right did the Sex Discrimination Act give women?
> 3 What things show that women have still not achieved complete equality?
> 4 What effect did the development of equal rights in other countries have on the UK?
>
> **Answers on page 111**

Topic 1.4.2 Christians and equal rights for women in religion

Revised

Many Evangelical Protestants teach that men and women have separate and different roles and so cannot have equal rights in religion. Women should not speak in church and only men can be Church leaders and teachers because:

● in the Bible, St Paul teaches that women should not teach or speak in church

● St Paul also uses the story of Adam and Eve in Genesis to show that men have been given more rights by God because Adam was created first

● although Jesus had women followers, he chose only men as his twelve apostles.

Many Protestant Churches (e.g. Church of England, Methodist, United Reformed Church, Baptist) give men and women equal rights, and have women ministers and priests, because:

● the creation story in Genesis 1 says that God created man and woman at the same time in his image and therefore they are of equal status

● in the New Testament, St Paul teaches that men and women are equal in Christ

● there is evidence from the Gospels that Jesus treated women as his equals.

The Catholic Church teaches that men and women should have equal rights in society and in religion, except that women cannot be deacons, priests or bishops, because:

● it is the teaching of the Catholic Catechism that men and women are equal, and should have equal rights in life and society

● only men can be priests because the apostles were all men, and priests and bishops are successors of the apostles

● only men can be priests because Jesus was a man and the priest represents Jesus in the Mass.

Evaluation of Christians and equal rights for women in religion

When arguing for women having equal rights in religion, use the reasons for the modern Protestant attitude and fact that the Catholic Catechism teaches that men and women are equal. For arguments against women having equal right in religion use the reasons for the Evangelical Protestant attitude and the reasons Catholics use to explain why deacons, priests and bishops should be men, all given above.

Common mistake

Some students write about the Catholic attitude as if it were the only Christian attitude and completely ignore the fact that there are women priests in the Protestant Churches.

Now test yourself

Tested

1 Which Christians think women cannot be priests or ministers?
2 Which Christians have women priests and ministers?
3 Who teaches, in the New Testament, that men and women are equal in Christ?
4 Why does the Catholic Mass mean that priests have to be men?

Answers on page 111

Topic 1.4.3 Muslims and equal rights for women in religion

If you have studied either Judaism, or Hinduism or Sikhism at school, you can find the revision notes for these on the website: **www.therevisionbutton.co.uk/myrevisionnotes**

Some Muslims (Traditionalists) believe that men and women should have different roles in life and religion, and therefore they should have different rights. They believe that women should perform their religious duties (except hajj) in the home and men should worship God in the mosque with their sons and lead the religion. The reasons Muslims think men and women should have different rights include the following:

- The Qur'an teaches that men should support women because God has given men a stronger physique.
- The Qur'an teaches that women have been created to bear children and men to provide for them.
- The Qur'an teaches that men need more money than women to be the family providers.
- It is traditional for only men to attend the mosque and to be imams.

Some Muslims (Modernists) believe that men and women should have completely equal rights in religion and education and a few would accept women religious leaders because:

- the Qur'an teaches that men and women are equal in religion and education
- there is evidence that Muhammad encouraged both men and women to worship in the mosque
- there were women religious leaders during the early stages of Islam
- they have been affected by the non-religious arguments for equal rights for women.

Many British Muslims mix these two attitudes and agree with women having equal rights in everything except religion.

Evaluation of Muslims and equal rights for women in religion

Evaluation questions will ask you to refer to only one religion, so it would be best just to use Christianity in answering evaluation questions, although you could use extra reasons from Islam.

> **Common mistake**
>
> Candidates often forget that some Muslims believe in equal rights for women, and this can lose them half the marks for a question.

Now test yourself

1 Where should women perform their religious duties according to those Muslims who believe men and women have different roles?
2 What teaches that men and women are equal in religion and education?
3 What claims that men and women should have different roles because God created men with a stronger physique?
4 Who encouraged both men and women to worship in the mosque?

Answers on page 111

Topic 1.4.4 The UK as a multi-ethnic society

The UK has always been an ethnically mixed society that has believed in human freedom and offered asylum to those suffering persecution. In the 2011 Census, 14 per cent of the UK's population came from **ethnic minorities**, and over half of these were born and educated in the UK.

Prejudice against certain ethnic groups leads to discrimination and **racism**, which can cause problems in a **multi-ethnic society** because:

- racially prejudiced employers might not give jobs to certain ethnic groups
- religiously prejudiced employers will not give jobs to certain religious groups
- prejudiced landlords are likely to refuse accommodation to certain ethnic groups or religions
- prejudiced teachers might discriminate against certain minorities and prevent them from achieving the results they should
- prejudiced police officers might discriminate against certain ethnic or religious groups by stopping and searching them when they have no real reason for so doing.

Prejudice and discrimination can have bad effects because if certain groups feel that they are being treated unfairly by society then they will begin to work against that society. Some politicians believe that some young black people turn to crime because they feel they will not be able to get good well-paid jobs because of discrimination. Some politicians believe that some young Muslims have been turning to extremist Islamic groups because they feel they have no chance of success in a prejudiced British society.

If a multi-ethnic society is to function well, it must treat all its members fairly and give equal opportunities to all its members.

Benefits of multi-ethnic societies

Multi-ethnic societies bring far more benefits than problems because:

- people of different ethnic groups and nationalities get to know and like each other, and intermarry
- multi-ethnic societies tend to be more advanced because new people bring in new ideas and new ways of doing things
- they help people to live and work in a world of multi-national companies and economic interdependence between all nations
- they make life more interesting with a much greater variety of food, music, fashion and entertainment.

Evaluation of the UK as a multi-ethnic society

People who argue against multi-ethnic societies use such arguments as:

- different ethnic groups living in one society are likely to come into conflict with each other
- each country should be occupied by only one ethnic group so it is their country
- multi-ethnic societies can lead to the loss of the culture of the original group (for example, one effect of non-Cornish ethnic groups living in Cornwall was the disappearance of the Cornish language)
- if every ethnic group had its own country, there would be no conflict.

Key terms

Ethnic minority – an ethnic group (race) which is much smaller than the majority group.

Prejudice – the belief that some people are inferior or superior without even knowing them.

Racism – the belief that some races are superior to others.

Multi-ethnic society – one in which many different races and cultures live together in one society.

Common mistake

Students often confuse multi-ethnic and multi-faith. Ethnic refers to race/culture; faith refers to religion.

Now test yourself

1. In the 2011 census, what percentage of the UK's population came from ethnic minorities?
2. What is it that causes people to discriminate against ethnic minorities?
3. What is thought to happen if groups of people think they are being unfairly treated by society?
4. Why do multi-ethnic societies tend to be more advanced?

Answers on page 111

Topic 1.4.5 Government action to promote community cohesion

A multi-ethnic society needs to promote **community cohesion** in order to remove the problems of prejudice, discrimination and racism. The British government promotes community cohesion by:

- appointing cabinet ministers, judges, etc, from ethnic minorities

- passing laws making it illegal to discriminate against anyone because of race, colour, nationality, ethnic or national origins

- passing laws making it illegal to stir up racial or religious hatred

- establishing the Equality and Human Rights Commission to get rid of discrimination and to build good relations.

Community cohesion is important for multi-ethnic and **multi-faith societies** because:

- without community cohesion different groups have different ideas about what society should be like and this can lead to violence such as racially/religiously motivated street rioting

- lack of community cohesion can lead people to lose their sense of allegiance (e.g. the 7 July 2005 London bombers were British-born Muslims)

- in countries without community cohesion violence becomes a way of life

- lack of community cohesion makes it impossible for people to co-operate in the way modern civilised living needs.

Evaluation of government action to promote community cohesion

You may be asked to argue for and against the need for/importance of government action to promote community cohesion.

1 For arguments for its importance use the reasons listed above.

2 Those who argue against government action to promote community cohesion are likely to use such arguments as:

- if people are forced to co-operate, it might lead to fighting and hatred of different groups

- the UK has always believed in multi-culturalism – allowing people from different ethnic and cultural backgrounds to live in the UK while following their own culture – which avoids conflict

- it does not matter if different cultural communities follow their own ideas about society as long as they all obey British laws.

> **Key terms**
>
> **Community cohesion** – a common vision and shared sense of belonging for all groups in society.
> **Multi-faith society** – many different religions living together in one society.

> **Exam tip**
>
> When answering questions on community cohesion, it is a good idea to begin by explaining what community cohesion is.

> **Now test yourself**
>
>
> 1 What is needed to remove the problems of prejudice, discrimination and racism?
> 2 What are the aims of the Equality and Human Rights Commission?
> 3 Name one example of the dangers of people losing their sense of allegiance to the society they live in.
> 4 What can happen if different groups have different ideas about what society should be like?
>
> **Answers on page 111**

Topic 1.4.6 Why Christians should promote racial harmony

Revised

Christians should try to promote (bring about) **racial harmony** because:

- in the parable of the Good Samaritan, Jesus showed that races who hated each other (like the Jews and Samaritans) should love each other as neighbours

- Jesus treated people of different races equally

- St Peter had a vision from God telling him not to discriminate because God has no favourites among the races

- St Paul taught that all races are equal in Christ since God created all races in his image

- the Christian Church has members from every race; over 50 per cent of the world is Christian and 70 per cent of Christians are non-white

- all the Christian Churches have made statements recently condemning any form of racism or racial discrimination.

Key term

Racial harmony – different races/colours living together happily.

Evaluation of why Christians should promote racial harmony

You are likely to be asked to argue for and against religion/Christianity being the best way to bring about racial harmony.

1 For reasons for the statement use the main points in this topic and the main points from the religion you are studying in Topic 1.4.7.

2 Arguments against religion/Christianity being the best way to bring about racial harmony could include such reasons as:

- some Christian groups work against racial harmony, for example the Ku Klux Klan

- politics is a better way of bringing about racial harmony, for example the USA now has a black president, but the Catholic Church does not have a black Pope

- not everyone is religious and so things like laws which give everyone equal rights are more likely to bring about racial harmony.

Exam tip

When answering evaluation questions on community cohesion or racism, you should always use religious reasons for promoting racial harmony.

Now test yourself

Tested

1 In which teaching did Jesus show that races who hated each other should love each other as neighbours?
2 Who had a vision from God telling him not to discriminate because God has no favourites among the races?
3 Who taught that all races are equal in Christ since God created all races in his image?
4 What percentage of Christians are non-white?

Answers on page 111

Topic 1.4.7 Why Muslims should promote racial harmony

If you have studied either Judaism, or Hinduism or Sikhism at school, you can find the revision notes for these on the website: **www.therevisionbutton.co.uk/myrevisionnotes**

It is important for Muslims to work for racial harmony because:

- the Qur'an teaches that God created the whole of humanity from one pair of humans, therefore all races are related and none can be regarded as superior

- in his final sermon, Muhammad said that every Muslim is a brother to every other Muslim, and so there should be no racism among Muslims

- Islam teaches that all Muslims form one brotherhood, the Ummah; this means that all Muslims, whatever their race, should regard each other as brothers and sisters

- Islam is against any form of racism and Muslim leaders and local mosques work with various groups to promote racial harmony in the UK.

Evaluation of why Muslims should promote racial harmony

Evaluation questions will ask you to refer to only one religion, so it would be best just to use Christianity in answering evaluation questions, although you could use extra reasons from Islam.

Now test yourself

1 What teaching from the Qur'an means that all races are related and none can be regarded as superior?

2 What did Muhammad teach about racism in his final sermon?

3 What Muslim ideal means that all Muslims, whatever their race, should regard each other as brothers and sisters?

4 How do Muslims show they are against any form of racism?

Answers on page 111

Topic 1.4.8 The UK as a multi-faith society

Many societies were mono-faith (having only one religion) until the twentieth century, but Britain has had believers of different faiths for many years and by the end of the twentieth century Muslims, Jews, Hindus, Sikhs, Buddhists and other religions were settled in the UK, so that it is a truly multi-faith society.

The benefits of living in a multi-faith society

The benefits of living in a multi-faith society include:

● People can learn about other religions and this can help them to see what religions have in common, leading to less prejudice.

● People from different religions may practise their religion more seriously and this may make people think about how they practise their own religion.

● People are likely to become more understanding about and respectful of each other's religions.

● **Religious freedom** and understanding will exist in a multi-faith society and this may help to stop religious conflicts.

● A multi-faith society may even make some people think more about religion as they come across religious ideas they have never thought about before.

Evaluation of the UK as a multi-faith society

You are likely to be asked to argue for and against living in a multi-faith society.

1 To argue for living in a multi-faith society, use the reasons listed under 'The benefits of living in a multi-faith society' above.

2 People who are firm believers in one religion might be against multi-faith societies because:

● they encourage your children to look at other religions, and your children might desert your religion

● children from different religions may want to marry each other, and **interfaith marriages** can create problems for religious parents

● they can make it difficult to follow your religion because society cannot be organised for every religion's different rules.

> ### Key terms
>
> **Religious freedom** – the right to practise your religion and change your religion.
>
> **Interfaith marriage** – marriage where the husband and wife are from different religions.

> ### Exam tip
>
> Make sure you use the key terms 'religious freedom' and 'religious pluralism' when answering questions on multi-faith society.

Now test yourself

1 What is a society called that only has one religion practised in it?
2 What does learning about other religions help people to do?
3 What is the danger religious people feel of their children learning about other religions?
4 What may religious freedom and understanding help to prevent?

Answers on page 111

Topic 1.4.9 Issues raised for religion by a multi-faith society

Revised

Conversion

Many religions see it as their duty to convert everyone because they believe that their religion is the only true religion and the only way to get to heaven; their holy books teach them that they should convert non-believers.

However, this raises problems because trying to convert other religions is a form of discrimination; it is impossible to say all other religions are wrong unless you have studied all of them. Trying to convert others can lead to arguments and even violence.

Bringing up children

A multi-faith society requires religious freedom and **religious pluralism** and children have to learn about the different religions in the society. This causes problems for many religious believers because parents want their children to become members of their religion and worry about what will happen to their children after death if they do not stay in their religion. They also worry that children educated in state schools will be tempted away from religious lifestyles.

Interfaith marriages

In a multi-faith society, young people of different faiths are going to meet, fall in love and want to marry. This can raise problems because they might not be able to have a religious wedding ceremony and the parents and relatives of the couple often feel that they have been betrayed.

Unless these issues are dealt with, then religion itself can work against community cohesion and promote conflict and hatred.

Evaluation of issues raised for religion by a multi-faith society

You may be asked to argue for and against having the right to bring up children in one faith only.

1 For arguments in favour of the right, use the reasons listed under 'Bringing up children' to the left.

2 The main arguments against children being brought up in one faith only include that:

- it is a human right to have freedom of religion and so children need to learn about more than one religion before they choose which to follow, or not follow

- a multi-faith society needs its members to respect all religions, and children need to learn about other religions if they are to respect the followers of that religion

- children who are brought up knowing only one religion cannot really believe it because they have not compared it with anything else, so they cannot know that it is the best religion.

You may be asked to argue for and against interfaith marriages.

1 The main arguments for interfaith marriages are that:

- it is a human right to be able to marry anyone you want to (especially if you are in love with them)

- interfaith marriages will encourage community cohesion as families from different faiths become one family

- the children of interfaith marriages will have true religious freedom as they learn about both their parents' religions and can choose between them.

2 For arguments against interfaith marriages use the reasons listed under 'Interfaith marriages' on this page.

Key term

Religious pluralism – accepting all religions as having an equal right to coexist.

Revised

Topic 1.4.10 Ways in which religion promotes community cohesion

1 Different religions are beginning to work with other religions to try to discover similarities between religions (for example, Judaism, Islam and Christianity believe in the prophets Abraham and Moses), and from this to work out ways of living together without trying to convert each other.

2 Some religious groups are developing ways of helping interfaith marriages and many Protestant Churches and Liberal or Reform Jewish synagogues have special wedding services for mixed-faith couples.

3 Leaders from the Church of England, Hindu, Sikh, Catholic, Muslim, Jewish and Buddhist faiths have agreed to follow the National Framework on Religious Education so that children in faith schools will now be taught the main religions practised in the UK.

4 The main way in which religions are trying to promote community cohesion is through working together in special groups such as the Inter Faith Network for the UK and local groups that bring together people of different faiths in the area.

Evaluation of ways in which religion promotes community cohesion

You may be asked to argue for and against whether religions are doing enough to promote community cohesion in the UK.

1 To argue that religions are doing enough to promote community cohesion in the UK use any of the points above.

2 Arguments that religions are not doing enough to promote community cohesion are that:

- all religions have groups that still teach that all other religions are wrong
- most religious people are unaware of what is going on with other faiths
- few religious believers look at the beliefs of other religions and try to work out which is true.

> **Common mistake**
>
> Students often mix up what religion is doing with what the government is doing to promote community cohesion.

Now test yourself

Tested

1 Which religions believe in the Prophets Abraham and Moses?
2 Which religions have special wedding services for interfaith couples?
3 What have leaders from the Church of England, Hindu, Sikh, Catholic, Muslim, Jewish and Buddhist faiths agreed to follow in faith schools?
4 Name a national UK religious group trying to promote community cohesion.

Answers on page 112

Topic 1.4.11 How the media deal with religion and community cohesion

You have to study how **one** issue from religion and community cohesion has been presented in **one** form of the media.

From your class notes you should have:

● notes on why the issue is important and why you think the producers decided to focus on this issue

● an outline of how the issue was presented, listing the main events and the way the events explored the issue

● notes on the way religious beliefs are treated in the presentation of the issue

● four pieces of evidence on whether you think the presentation was fair to religious beliefs

● notes on the way religious people are treated in the presentation

● four pieces of evidence on whether you think the presentation was fair to religious people.

Evaluation of how the media deal with religion and community cohesion

Although you are unlikely to be asked an evaluation question on this topic, if you were it would be about whether the media treats religious beliefs or people fairly.

1 To argue for fair treatment you should use:

● the evidence you have from your form of the media for the religious beliefs being treated fairly

● the evidence you have from your form of the media for religious people being treated fairly.

2 To argue against fair treatment you should use:

● the evidence you have from your form of the media for the religious beliefs not being treated fairly

● the evidence you have from your form of the media for religious people not being treated fairly.

> **Common mistake**
>
> Students often simply describe the film/programme. You only receive marks for explaining whether the treatment was fair.

> **Exam tip**
>
> Make sure that you identify the film or TV programme you are writing about.

> **Now test yourself**
>
>
> 1 What film/programme are you revising?
> 2 What issue is being dealt with?
> 3 How many pieces of evidence do you need for the treatment being fair to religion?
> 4 How many pieces of evidence do you need for the treatment not being fair to religion?
>
> **Answers on page 112**

Exam practice

Answer both questions

1 a) What is an ethnic minority? (2 marks)

   b) Do you think men and women should have equal roles in life? Give two reasons for your point of view. (4 marks)

   c) Explain why racism and discrimination bring problems to a multi-ethnic society. (8 marks)

   d) 'It is easy for different religions to work together in the UK.'

     (i) Do you agree? Give reasons for your opinion. (3 marks)

     (ii) Give reasons why some people may disagree with you. (3 marks)

     In your answer you should refer to at least one religion.

                                             (Total: 20 marks)

2 a) What is interfaith marriage? (2 marks)

   b) Do you think Christians should work for racial harmony? Give two reasons for your point of view. (4 marks)

   c) Explain how the government is working to promote community cohesion in the UK. (8 marks)

   d) 'If everyone were religious, there would be no racism.'

     (i) Do you agree? Give reasons for your opinion. (3 marks)

     (ii) Give reasons why some people may disagree with you. (3 marks)

     In your answer you should refer to at least one religion.

                                             (Total: 20 marks)

Summary

- Attitudes to the roles of men and women have changed greatly as women now have equal rights and men and women are expected to share roles in the home. Attitudes have changed because of the feminist movement, social and industrial changes and the effects of the world wars.

- Evangelical Protestants believe only men should be religious leaders because this is what the Bible teaches. Liberal Protestants believe men and women should have equal rights in religion because Jesus had women disciples. Catholics believe men and women should have equal rights, but only men can become priests because Jesus was a man.

- Traditional Muslims believe that men and women should have different rights in religion because of tradition and the teachings of the Qur'an. Modern Muslims believe that men and women should have equal rights in religion because of the teachings of the Qur'an and the example of the Prophet.

- Britain has many ethnic minorities and so is a multi-ethnic society. Multi-ethnic societies have many benefits, such as advancing more quickly because they have a greater variety of ideas. A multi-ethnic society needs equal opportunities and treatment to work, so prejudice and discrimination cause major problems in such a society because not everyone is treated equally.

- The UK government is promoting community cohesion by passing laws against racism and discrimination and making community cohesion part of the national curriculum. Community cohesion is important because without it a multi-ethnic society will become violent and divided.

- Christians should promote racial harmony because of the teachings of the Bible and the Churches against racism, and the example of Jesus. Muslims should promote racial harmony because Islam teaches that racism is wrong because of the teachings of the Qur'an and the example of Muhammad.

- Britain is a multi-faith society because several religions are practised here and everyone is free to practise their religion. A multi-faith society has many benefits, such as religious freedom and the opportunity to find out about, and think more deeply about, different religions. A multi-faith society needs to have laws giving equal rights to all religions and to those who have no religion (religious pluralism).

- A multi-faith society can raise problems for religious people in areas such as:
  - trying to convert other faiths, because it is like discrimination
  - bringing up children, because they may leave their parents' faith
  - interfaith marriages, because of having to decide which faith the children should be brought up in.

- Religions are working for community cohesion in the UK by:
  - working to discover what is the same about religions
  - helping with interfaith marriages
  - making sure that all children learn about different faiths
  - joining local and national groups to promote community cohesion.

- When studying the presentation of an issue from religion and community cohesions in the media, you must be able to explain: why the issue was chosen, how it was presented, whether the presentation treated religious beliefs and people fairly.

Section 1 Religion: rights and responsibilities

Topic 8.1.1 Why some Christians use only the Bible as a basis for moral decisions

Revised

Moral decisions are when you have to decide what is the right or wrong thing to do.

1. Many Christians use only the **Bible** when making a moral decision because:

   - they believe the Bible is the word of God and so is God's guidance on making decisions
   - the Bible contains the **Decalogue** which gives guidance on such things as the treatment of parents, stealing, murder, adultery, lying, etc.
   - the Bible contains the teachings of Jesus on how to live, which Christians should follow since they believe Jesus is the Son of God
   - the Bible contains letters from the leading disciples of Jesus about how Christians should behave.

2. Some Christians do not think the Bible is the most important guide to making moral decisions because:

   - some Christians believe that the Bible was written by humans inspired by God, so many of its attitudes need to be changed for the modern world (for example, St Paul's attitude to women and slaves)
   - some Christians believe they need the **Church** to tell them what the Bible means for today
   - other Christians would use their own **conscience** or reason to decide whether to follow the Bible today.

Evaluation of why some Christians use only the Bible

You may be required to argue for and against the Bible being the most important guide for making moral decisions.

1. To argue for, you should use part 1 above on why many Christians use only the Bible.

2. To argue against you could use part 2 above on why some Christians do not think the Bible is the most important guide.

> **Key terms**
>
> **Bible** – the holy book of Christians, comprising the Old and New Testaments
>
> **Decalogue** – another name for the Ten Commandments.
>
> **Church** – the community of Christians ('church' with a small 'c' means a Christian place of worship).
>
> **Conscience** – an inner feeling of the rightness or wrongness of an action.

> **Exam tip**
>
> If you are asked why some Christians use the Bible for making moral decisions, make sure you give all four of the reasons given in part 1 above.

Now test yourself

Tested

1. What is the Decalogue?
2. Why should Christians follow the teachings of Jesus?
3. What do the letters from the disciples give Christians guidance about?
4. What do some Christians think they need to tell them what the Bible means for today?

Answers on page 112

Topic 8.1.2 The authority of the Church for Christians

Although the Bible is the basic guide for Christian decision-making, most Christians believe that only the Church can explain what the Bible means for Christians today because:

● they believe the Church is the Body of Christ – Jesus working in today's world – so it must have the same authority as Christ

● most Christians believe that God speaks to the world today through the Church

● the Church is guided by God in making decisions on today's moral issues

● following the guidance of the Church stops Christians from being confused about what to do, and means Christians can be sure they are doing the right thing

● Catholic Christians believe that the Magisterium (the Pope and the bishops interpreting the Bible and tradition for Catholics today) gives perfect guidance on moral behaviour.

Evaluation of the authority of the Church for Christians

You may be required to argue for and against the teaching of the Church being the best guide for Christians to make moral decisions.

1 To argue that the Church is the best guide, you should use the reasons above.

2 To argue against, you could use the reasons why some Christians think the Bible is more important (page 53), and/or conscience (page 55) and/or Situation Ethics (page 56).

> **Common mistake**
>
> Students often spell the Church with a small 'c'. This annoys examiners. The Church always needs a capital 'c'. With a small 'c' it's just the building.

> **Exam tip**
>
> Use specific facts and specialist vocabulary wherever possible; for example, don't just say 'the Catholic Church's teaching', say, 'the teaching of the Magisterium'.

> **Now test yourself** ──────────────── Tested
>
> 1 What does it mean when Christians call the Church 'the Body of Christ'?
> 2 How does God speak to today's world, according to many Christians?
> 3 What stops Christians from being confused about what to do?
> 4 What name is given to the Pope and the bishops interpreting the Bible and tradition for Catholics today?
>
> **Answers on page 112**

Topic 8.1.3 Why some Christians believe conscience is the best guide for making moral decisions

All humans have a conscience which makes them feel guilty if they do things which they think are wrong.

1 Some Christians believe they should follow the guidance of the Bible and the Church, but if this conflicts with what their conscience says, they should follow their conscience because:

- the voice of conscience is an inner voice which seems to be the same as the voice of God, therefore Christians should follow it
- the Church says that Christians should follow their conscience as if it were the voice of God
- St Paul and St Thomas Aquinas taught that Christians should use their conscience as the final part of moral decision-making
- the Bible often needs to be interpreted, the teachings of the Church come through people, but conscience is God speaking directly to individuals.

2 Some Christians think they should not always follow their conscience because:

- people have heard the voice of God telling them to do bad things; if people can be mistaken about the voice of God, they could be mistaken about the voice of conscience
- if Christians follow the teachings of the Bible they are doing what all Christians agree is the Christian thing to do
- if Christians follow the teachings of the Church, they are doing what other Christians think is right
- if everyone followed their conscience rather than laws, there would be chaos as no one would know what sort of behaviour to expect from each other.

Evaluation of why some Christians believe conscience is the best guide

You may be required to argue for and against following your conscience as the best way to make moral decisions.

1 To argue for you should use the reasons in part 1 above for why some Christians believe they should follow their conscience.

2 To argue against you should use the reasons in part 2 above for why some Christians think they should not always follow their conscience.

Exam tip

When answering the b) questions, make sure that you develop each reason so you get full marks.

Now test yourself ——————————————— Tested

1 What is conscience?
2 Some Christians think their conscience is the same as the voice of whom?
3 Which saints said that Christians should use their conscience as the final part of moral decision-making?
4 Why would there be chaos if everyone followed their conscience rather than laws?

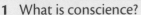
Answers on page 112

Topic 8.1.4 Why some Christians think Situation Ethics is the best guide for making moral decisions

Situation Ethics is the idea that Christians should base moral decisions on what is the most loving thing to do in any situation needing a moral decision. For example, the Bible says that stealing is wrong, so it would be wrong to steal nuclear weapons from a madman, but Situation Ethics would say a Christian should steal the nuclear weapons because that would be the most loving thing for society.

1 Some Christians think Situation Ethics is the best guide because:

- Jesus seemed to follow Situation Ethics because he overruled what the Old Testament said when he thought it was unloving; for example, Jesus healed people on the Sabbath because he said it was more important to do good than to obey the Sabbath laws

- Jesus said the greatest commandments are to love God and love your neighbour, meaning Christians should always do what will have the most loving results

- Christianity is a religion of love and so Christians should make their moral decisions based on love not laws

- they think it is wrong to ignore the consequences of your actions, so Christians should always do what produces the best results.

2 Some Christians think Situation Ethics is wrong because:

- they believe the Bible is God's word to Christians about how to live, so it should be the basis for moral decision-making

- they believe Christians should follow the Ten Commandments and the Sermon on the Mount rather than relying on their own ideas

- they claim you can never be sure of the consequences of a choice because you can never know you have all the facts of the situation, therefore it is better to follow the rules of the Church and/or Bible.

Evaluation of why some Christians think Situation Ethics is the best guide

You may be asked to argue for and against Christians basing their moral decisions on the most loving thing to do.

1 To argue for Christians basing their moral decisions on Situation Ethics, you should use the reasons given in part 1 above for why some Christians use Situation Ethics as a guide for making moral decisions.

2 To argue against, you should use the reasons in part 2 above for why some Christians think Situation Ethics is wrong.

> **Key term**
>
> **Situation Ethics** – the idea that Christians should base moral decisions on what is the most loving thing to do.

> **Exam tip**
>
> When answering evaluation questions, make sure you state your opinion, give **three** reasons for it and then give **three** reasons why some people may disagree with you.

> **Now test yourself**
>
> 1 What does Situation Ethics say Christians should base their moral decisions on?
> 2 Who overruled what the Old Testament said when he thought it was unloving?
> 3 What did Jesus say are the two greatest commandments?
> 4 Why do some Christians think the Bible should be the basis of Christian moral decision-making?
>
> **Answers on page 112**

Topic 8.1.5 Why some Christians use a variety of authorities to make moral decisions

When faced with actual decisions, Christians often find it easier and more useful to use two or three of the Christian guidance authorities. For example:

● Protestants might usually use the Bible as their authority because it is straightforward to use, for example: do not steal, do not murder. However, it is more difficult for modern issues such as contraception or civil partnerships. The Bible says nothing about contraception or civil partnerships, so they would have to look to the teaching of the Church or their conscience for guidance.

● Catholics would normally follow the authority of the Church, as the Magisterium applies the teachings of the Bible and the apostles to modern life. However, they might feel unable to follow it on some complex modern issues (for example, supplying condoms to African states with high rates of AIDS or encouraging civil partnerships) and turn to Situation Ethics or conscience.

● A Christian who usually followed their conscience might turn to the authority of the Bible or the Church if what their conscience was telling them went against what they knew was accepted Christian teaching. A good example would be if a Christian heard the voice of God telling them to kill all doctors who perform abortions. The Bible and the Church say that it is wrong to murder whatever the reasons. So they would use the authority of the Bible or the Church to reject the voice of their conscience.

● A Christian who usually used Situation Ethics might decide that the issue was so complicated and the effects of a choice so uncertain that the safest thing would be to follow either the authority of the Bible or the authority of the Church because they are more likely to give the right choice than an individual trying to work it all out for themselves.

> **Exam tip**
>
> If asked to explain why some Christians use a variety of authorities when making a moral decision, make sure you use all four reasons given on this page to gain a level 4.

Now test yourself

Tested

1 Why might it be difficult for Christians to use the Bible alone for modern issues such as contraception or civil partnerships?
2 What applies the teachings of the Bible and the apostles to modern life for Catholics?
3 When might a Christian who usually followed their conscience turn to the authority of the Bible or the Church?
4 If the issue was so complicated and the effects of a choice so uncertain, what might a follower of Situation Ethics use instead?

Answers on page 112

Topic 8.1.6 Human rights in the UK

Revised

In 1998, the **Human Rights** Act was passed, giving UK citizens the right to:

● life, liberty and a fair trial

● freedom from torture and slavery

● respect for private and family life

● freedom of thought, conscience and religion and freedom to express their views

● meet with others to discuss their views and to organise public demonstrations to publicise their views

● marry or form a civil partnership and start a family

● own property and have an education

● take part in free elections.

If any of these rights and freedoms are abused you have a right to go to court, even if the abuse was by someone in authority like a police officer.

Clearly, by having such rights, all UK citizens have a duty to respect the rights of others.

Evaluation of human rights in the United Kingdom

You may be required to argue for and against human rights being important.

1   To argue for human rights being important, you could use such reasons as:

● without human rights such as the right to liberty and a fair trial, you could find yourself living in a dictatorship because all opposition leaders have been imprisoned

● without the right to freedom of thought and freedom of expression, minority religions and minority political parties could be banned

● without the right to take part in free elections, there would be no democracy.

2   To argue against human rights being important, you could use such reasons as:

● people abuse human rights laws; for example, prisoners claiming that their punishment infringes their human rights

● in a democracy you don't need special human rights because people can vote for what they want

● you ought to be able to torture terrorists to find out information that would save innocent lives; for example, to find out where they have planted bombs.

> **Key term**
>
> **Human rights** – the rights and freedoms to which everyone is entitled.

> **Common mistake**
>
> Students sometimes argue that human rights come from religion when they actually come from politics and the UN.

Now test yourself

Tested

1   What is it that gives UK citizens human rights?

2   One right is the right to life, liberty and what?

3   Another right is freedom of thought, conscience and what?

4   What can you do if your rights or freedoms are abused?

Answers on page 112

Topic 8.1.7 Why human rights are important for Christians

1 Christians believe that human rights are important because:

- the right to life is a basic Christian belief because of the belief that life is holy and belongs to God (sanctity of life).

- Christians believe that all people are made in the image of God and so are one human family; therefore it is important to Christians that everyone is treated fairly and equally, which human rights ensure.

- freedom of thought, conscience and religion, freedom of expression, freedom of assembly and association are part of being Christian; Christians must have the legal right to believe in Christianity, share their beliefs with others and meet together for worship.

- it is also an essential human right for Christians not to be disadvantaged compared to others, since it means that employers cannot discriminate against Christians over jobs and pay. For example, employers cannot refuse to employ Christians because they don't want religious people in the workplace.

2 However, human rights can cause problems for Christians because:

- many Christians are against the right to form civil partnerships because they believe that homosexuality is against God's will

- some Christians are against the right to marry a person from a different faith; they believe Christians should only marry Christians so that the children are brought up as Christians

- some Christians are against the right of homosexuals to raise a family; they believe that children should be brought up by a mother and a father

- human rights laws could be used to argue for the right for women to become priests, or the right of priests to marry.

Evaluation of why human rights are important for Christians

You may be required to argue for and against human rights being important for Christians.

1 To argue for, you could use the reasons for human rights being important given in part 1 above.

2 To argue against, you could use the reasons for human rights causing problems for Christians given in part 2 above.

Exam tip

To answer evaluation questions on human rights, you need to know why some Christians have problems with human rights.

Now test yourself

Tested

1 Why is the right to life a basic Christian belief?
2 Why is it important to Christians that everyone is treated fairly and equally?
3 Why are some Christians against the right to form civil partnerships?
4 Why are some Christians against the right to marry a person from a different faith?

Answers on page 112

Topic 8.1.8 Why people should take part in electoral and democratic processes

The UK is a democracy so every UK citizen over the age of eighteen is entitled to vote for MPs, local councillors, MEPs and to be a candidate in any of these elections. Every citizen also has the right to try to change the policies of the government, council or European Union (EU) by joining or forming a **political party** or **pressure group** or having a meeting with their MP, councillor or MEP.

It is important to take part in **electoral** and **democratic processes** because:

- you pay income tax on your wages and VAT on what you buy, and voting gives you some control over how much this is and how it is spent

- local councils set the level of the council tax you have to pay, so voting gives you some control over how much this is and how it is spent

- the European Parliament has some control over EU spending, so it is important to vote in European elections as it gives you some control over how money is spent

- taking part in electoral processes and democratic processes gives you a chance to affect new laws which may be passed

- the national government is responsible for important things like the armed forces, schools, the NHS, benefits and pensions; voting gives you a say in how these are run

- local councils are responsible for such things as refuse disposal, leisure and cultural services, trading standards, social services, housing services, maintaining the roads, etc. These are important areas that you need to have a say in.

Key terms

Political party – a group which tries to be elected into power on the basis of its policies (e.g. Labour, Conservative).

Pressure group – a group formed to influence government policy on a particular issue.

Electoral processes – the ways in which voting is organised.

Democratic processes – the ways in which all citizens can take part in government (usually through elections).

Exam tip

Make sure you do not confuse the areas national government is responsible for with the areas local government is responsible for.

Evaluation of why people should take part in electoral and democratic processes

You may be required to argue for and against it being important to take part in electoral processes (vote in elections/join or form a political party/stand as a candidate in elections).

1 To argue for it being important to take part in electoral and democratic processes, you could use the reasons above.

2 To argue against you could use such reasons as:

- one vote makes no difference to the outcome as there are over 60 million people in the UK

- all politicians make promises they don't keep so they are not worth voting for

- it doesn't matter who is voted in, they will just have to do what the EU says.

Now test yourself

1 How old do you have to be to vote in elections in the UK?
2 What tax do you have to pay on your wages?
3 Who is responsible for the NHS?
4 Who is responsible for refuse disposal?

Answers on page 112

Topic 8.1.9 Christian teachings on moral duties and responsibilities

Revised

Most Christians believe that they should take part in electoral and democratic processes, but that they should be guided by Christian teachings such as the following.

The Golden Rule

The Golden Rule taught by Jesus is: 'So in everything, do to others what you would have them do to you, for this sums up the Law and the Prophets' (Matthew 7:12).

Christians must use the Golden Rule when voting. For example, if a party wanted to send all asylum seekers back to their home country, a Christian would have to think, 'If I were a member of an ethnic group being slaughtered in my home country would I want to be sent back there?'

Jesus' parable of the Sheep and the Goats

'At the end of the world, the Son of Man will judge everyone. Like a shepherd, he will separate the sheep from goats. The sheep will be those who fed Jesus when he was hungry, gave him drink when he was thirsty, took him in when he was a stranger, clothed him when he needed clothes, looked after him when he was sick, visited him when he was in prison and they will go to heaven.

'However, the goats will be told that as they did not do any of these things for other people, they will go to hell.' (Adapted from Matthew 25:31–46.)

This parable shows it is the duty of Christians to help the poor and suffering by taking part in politics. For example, if a party's policy was to cut off benefits to the jobless who refused jobs, a Christian might accept this because they would not refuse work if they were jobless, but they would also have to think about the effects of the policy on the children of the jobless.

The teaching of St John on 'Am I my brother's keeper?'

In Genesis 4, Adam's son Cain is jealous of his brother Abel and murders him. When God asks Cain where his brother is, Cain replies, 'I don't know. Am I my brother's keeper?'. God then punishes Cain, showing that God created humans to be their brothers' keepers; that is, to look after each other.

This is explained more fully by St John, who says: 'We should love one another. Do not be like Cain who … murdered his brother … If anyone had material possessions and sees his brother in need but has no pity on him, how can the love of God be in him?' (1 John 3:11–18.)

These Christian teachings on being our brother's keeper show Christians that they have a duty to look after everyone in need, and work for **social change** so that society becomes truly Christian.

Evaluation of Christian teachings on moral duties and responsibilities

You may be required to argue for and against it being important for Christians to be guided by Christian teachings when taking part in democratic and electoral processes.

1 To argue for, you could use the comments on the Golden Rule, the Sheep and the Goats and 'Am I my brother's keeper?' given to the left and above.

2 To argue against you could use such reasons as:

- Christians don't need to take part in electoral processes because Jesus said that loving God is the greatest commandment, so it is more important to love God than take part in electoral processes

- going to Mass every Sunday is more important than taking part in electoral processes

- Christianity is about loving God, elections are about politics and the two should not mix.

Topic 8.1.10 The nature of genetic engineering

Genetic engineering is using techniques of gene development to find cures or prevention for disease and disabilities in humans. Scientists are involved in genetic research into diseases such as cystic fibrosis, muscular dystrophy and Huntington's chorea.

Most genetic research has been based on changing the cells that transmit information from one generation to the next (germline gene therapy) and removing defective genes from embryos. More recently, cloning processes have been used to grow healthy cells to replace the diseased ones using stem cells from embryos produced for in-vitro fertilisation (IVF) but not used, or from adult bone marrow or blood.

Non-religious arguments in favour of genetic engineering

Non-religious arguments in favour of genetic engineering include that:

● it offers the prospect of cures for currently incurable diseases

● it is being done in other countries and so is available to those rich enough to travel and pay for treatments

● cloning using animal eggs, as in cybrids (a human cell nucleus implanted into an animal cell where the nucleus has been removed), does not involve any loss of human life

● genetic research is closely monitored by the law, but has vast potential benefits.

Non-religious arguments against genetic engineering

Non-religious arguments against genetic engineering include that:

● there is too little information about the long-term consequences

● it has effects which can't be changed, so if anything went wrong it would be permanent

● it places too much power in the hands of scientists who could produce scientifically created human beings

● it treats the human body as no different from plants.

Genetic research in the UK is controlled by the law and by the Human Fertilisation and Embryology Authority (HFEA).

> **Common mistake**
>
> Students sometimes write about genetic engineering in plants, but this course is only about genetic engineering in medicine.

Now test yourself

1 Name two diseases genetic research is trying to find cures for.

2 What processes are used to grow healthy cells to replace the diseased ones using stem cells?

3 What is a human nucleus in an empty animal cell known as?

4 What is genetic research monitored by?

Answers on page 112

Topic 8.1.11 Different Christian attitudes to genetic engineering and cloning

There are several attitudes to genetic engineering among Christians:

1 **Liberal Protestants** support genetic engineering because:

   ● Jesus showed that Christians should do all they can to cure disease

   ● they think finding genetic cures is no different from finding drug cures

   ● they think there is a difference between creating cells and creating human embryos

   ● they do not think embryos become a foetus until they are fourteen days old.

2 **Roman Catholics, and some other Christians**, agree with genetic research as long as it does not involve the use of embryos because:

   ● they believe life begins at the moment of conception, whether in a womb or a test-tube, and killing life is wrong

   ● they believe killing an embryo is killing human life

   ● they believe that embryos have been produced by un-Christian means (for example, male masturbation).

3 **Some Christians** are against all genetic research because:

   ● they believe that God creates the genetic make-up of each person at conception and people have no right to interfere with this

   ● they believe genetic research is trying to play God, which is a great sin

   ● they believe it is wrong to try to make Earth perfect – only heaven is perfect.

Evaluation of different Christian attitudes to genetic engineering and cloning

You may be required to argue for and against genetic research.

1 To argue for, you should use the reasons why Liberal Protestants agree with genetic research given in part 1 above.

2 To argue against, you should use Catholic reasons and the reasons why some Christians are against all genetic research given in parts 2 and 3 above.

> **Exam tip**
>
> Remember that not all Christians are against genetic research. Liberal Protestants support it.

Now test yourself

Tested

1 Which Christians support genetic research?
2 Who showed that Christians should do all they can to cure disease?
3 Which Christians are against genetic research using embryos?
4 Some Christians believe the genetic make-up of each person is created at conception by whom?

Answers on page 112

Exam practice

Answer both questions

1 a) What is the Golden Rule? **(2 marks)**

   b) Do you think you are your brother's keeper? Give two reasons for your point of view. **(4 marks)**

   c) Explain why some Christians use Situation Ethics as a guide for making moral decisions. **(8 marks)**

   d) 'No Christian should use genetic engineering.'

   (i) Do you agree? Give reasons for your opinion. **(3 marks)**

   (ii) Give reasons why some people may disagree with you. **(3 marks)**

   In your answer you should refer to Christianity.

   (Total: 20 marks)

2 a) What is social change? **(2 marks)**

   b) Do you think the teachings of the Church are important for making moral decisions? Give two reasons for your point of view. **(4 marks)**

   c) Explain why human rights are important for Christians. **(8 marks)**

   d) 'It doesn't matter whether or not you vote.'

   (i) Do you agree? Give reasons for your opinion. **(3 marks)**

   (ii) Give reasons why some people may disagree with you. **(3 marks)**

   In your answer you should refer to Christianity.

   (Total: 20 marks)

Summary

- Some Christians would use only the Bible when making moral decisions because they believe that God speaks through the Bible. The Bible records God's teaching on how to behave and what Jesus taught about morality.

- Some Christians use the authority of the Church when making moral decisions because Church leaders are in the best position to say what the Bible means for today, and they always give guidance on moral issues. Catholic Christians believe the Pope and the bishops have special powers in interpreting the Bible.

- Conscience is the inner feeling that makes people think something is right or wrong. Many Christians think conscience is the way God speaks to Christians today and so is the main guide for making moral decisions. Other Christians think it is safer to follow the Bible or the Church.

- Situation Ethics is the idea that the only moral rule Christians need is to love your neighbour. Christians who follow this believe that all they need to do when faced with a moral decision is work out what is the most loving thing to do in that situation. Other Christians think this can cause problems because you can never know all the facts or all the consequences of your actions.

- Citizens of the UK have certain basic rights to make sure they are treated fairly and equally – the right to life, the right to liberty, the right to a fair trial, the right to freedom of conscience and religion, the right to marry and start a family, the right to an education, the right to take part in free elections.

- All human rights are important to Christians because they believe that all people are made in the image of God and so should have the same rights. They are also important because Christians believe in the sanctity of life and so all life belongs to God. However, some rights can cause problems for Christians; for example, when homosexuals want a civil partnership or women want to have equal rights in religion.

- It is important for people to vote in elections and be involved in politics because it gives them a chance to choose and affect governments and councils. These can have a big influence because they set taxes, pass new laws and run organisations like the NHS, and people should have a say in how this is done.

- Most Christians believe that they should take part in electoral and democratic processes guided by Christian teachings such as the Golden Rule, the parable of the Sheep and the Goats, and the story of Cain and Abel.

- Genetic engineering is finding out which genes cause diseases, such as muscular dystrophy, and then working out how the genes can be changed (often by cloning) so that the disease does not develop. Genetic research in the UK is controlled by the law and by the Human Fertilisation and Embryology Authority. Some Christians allow all genetic research, as long as it is to find cures for diseases, because Jesus was a healer. Some Christians allow genetic research which does not involve the destruction of embryos, which they believe to be human life. Some Christians oppose all genetic research because they believe it is 'playing God'.

Section 2 Religion: environmental and medical issues

Topic 8.2.1 Global warming – its causes and possible solutions

Revised

Global warming means that the Earth is warmer than it has been for over a thousand years, which could lead to some coastal areas disappearing, and countries such as Spain becoming deserts.

Most scientists believe that global warming is caused by the greenhouse effect. Burning fossil fuels (gas, coal and oil) produces carbon dioxide, which creates a barrier in the atmosphere rather like the glass in a greenhouse, so that the sun's heat can get through but cannot get back out again, making the Earth's temperature rise. We are now burning far more fossil fuels, therefore the Earth's temperature is rising.

Some scientists claim it is a result of natural changes because the warmest periods in the last 10,000 years happened well before the burning of fossil fuels. They claim that if the greenhouse effect were true, the troposphere would be heating up faster than the Earth's surface, but it does not seem to be.

Some scientists claim that changes in the Earth's temperature are caused by the amount of radiation coming from the sun. When solar activity is high, fewer clouds form so more of the sun's heat reaches the Earth and it warms up.

Possible solutions

Scientists claim we could reduce the greenhouse effect by:

- using wind power, sea power, hydroelectric power and solar power to produce electricity without producing carbon dioxide
- using ethanol, biodiesel, electric batteries and hydrogen to power cars without producing carbon emissions
- improving the efficiency and reducing the pollution caused by cars and lorries (new methods mean that

the total tonnage of pollutants emitted by cars is now 75 per cent less than twenty years ago)

- increasing the use of public transport (trains are by far the lowest carbon emission form of transport).

Evaluation of global warming

You may be required to argue for and against carbon emissions being the main cause of global warming.

1 To argue for carbon emissions being the main cause of global warming, you could use the points given to the left on the greenhouse effect.

2 To argue against carbon emissions being the main cause of global warming, you could use the points on natural climate change and solar activity.

You may be asked whether science can solve the problem of global warming.

1 To argue for science being able to solve the problem you could use the possible solutions given above.

2 To argue against science being able to solve the problem, you could use such points as:

- renewable energy sources for power stations are expensive and unreliable
- biofuels (ethanol and biodiesel) are produced from crops which could be used for food
- electric car batteries rely on electricity produced by power stations using oil or coal.

> **Key term**
>
> **Global warming** – the increase in the temperature of the Earth's atmosphere (thought to be caused by the greenhouse effect).

Now test yourself ──────── Tested

1 What do most scientists believe is the cause of global warming?
2 What should be heating up faster than the Earth's surface if there were a greenhouse effect?
3 What causes fewer clouds to form and more of the sun's heat to reach the Earth?
4 How can you produce electricity without increasing carbon emissions?

Answers on page 112

> **Exam tip**
>
> Evaluation questions on global warming don't often require you to refer to religion. Read the question carefully and, if it does not say 'in your answer you must refer to at least one religion', you will be able to answer using just the information on this page.

Topic 8.2.2 Forms of pollution and their possible solutions

Acid rain

Buildings and forests in countries such as Sweden and Germany are being destroyed by acid rain coming from the UK. This is caused by the burning of fossil fuels, which releases chemicals into the atmosphere and changes the pH of the rainwater in clouds, making it so acidic that it can burn things when it falls to Earth.

Waste

The waste produced by humans in the form of sewage, refuse (rubbish put into bins) and litter (rubbish left on the streets) is a major threat to the future of the planet. Europe produces more than 2.5 billion tonnes of solid waste a year. Untreated sewage causes water pollution and eutrophication (see below). Litter has led to a huge increase in the rat population, bringing many diseases to humans.

Eutrophication

Fertilisers being washed into streams, sewage pollution and a lack of trees to soak up nitrogen cause eutrophication by causing water plants to grow rapidly, using up all of the oxygen in the water, which causes fish and other aquatic life to die. This could lead to major health problems for humans, as poisons enter the water supply.

Radioactive pollution

Nuclear power stations are carbon-free, but produce radioactive pollution which will take thousands if not millions of years to be safe. Radioactive pollution causes death, cancers and genetic mutations.

Possible solutions

● The solution to acid rain is to create electricity from renewable sources. The problems of waste could be solved by a combination of recycling, using solid waste to produce electricity and using sewage to produce methane gas.

● The problem of litter would be solved if people stopped dropping litter; the UK has laws to punish litterers and to force local councils to clear littered areas.

● Better sewage treatment, fewer phosphates in detergents and fewer nitrates in farm fertilisers could stop eutrophication.

● Nuclear waste can be reprocessed so that 97 per cent of the waste can be re-used. However, the remaining 3 per cent of waste has to be stored and the UK government plans to isolate the waste in suitable rock formations ensuring no radioactivity ever reaches the surface.

Evaluation of forms of pollution and their possible solutions

You may be required to argue for and against the problems of pollution being able to be solved.

1 To argue for the problems of pollution being solvable, use the possible solutions above and the possible solutions to global warming (page 66).

2 To argue against the problems of pollution being solvable, you could use such reasons as:
  ● carbon emissions are set to double between 2010 and 2050 so any action is only likely to limit the rise, not stop it
  ● recycling is not working as the costs of recycling are so high and recycling glass bottles uses more energy than making new
  ● organic farming uses manure as fertiliser, causing an increase of nitrates in streams and rivers, increasing the risk of eutrophication.

Exam tip

Remember: carbon emissions are also a form of pollution.

Now test yourself

Tested

1 What is destroying buildings and forests in countries such as Sweden and Germany?
2 What is caused by fertilisers being washed into streams, sewage pollution and a lack of trees to soak up nitrogen?
3 What type of pollution do nuclear power stations produce?
4 What problem could be solved by a combination of recycling and using solid waste to produce electricity and sewage to produce methane gas?

Answers on page 113

Topic 8.2.3 The scarcity of natural resources

Natural resources are naturally occurring materials, such as oil and fertile land. Some are renewable resources that can be used over and over again, such as wind power, solar power, water power and fertile land. Others are finite or non-renewable resources that disappear once they are used, such as oil, coal, iron, tin, copper, uranium and natural gas.

Human use of finite resources causes major problems. For example, if oil is used up, we will not only have nothing to power cars, but all plastics and road surfaces, most candles, polishes and chemical foodstuffs come from oil. Use of metals causes similar problems: everything from car panels to kitchen appliances comes from finite resources such as iron, aluminium and tin. Many scientists feel that unless we stop using these resources at the current rate they will soon run out, causing problems as serious as global warming and pollution.

> **Key term**
>
> **Natural resources** – naturally occurring materials, such as oil and fertile land, which can be used by humans.

Possible solutions

- One solution would be to use renewable resources to make electricity; for example, nuclear, wind, sea, hydroelectric or solar power.

- Car manufacturers are looking at using water, sugar cane and electric batteries as ways of powering cars.

- Recycling will enable the lifetime of many finite resources to be extended and some cars are now made of almost 75 per cent recycled materials. Scientists are working on using chemicals from plants to produce plastics.

- Some people think an alternative lifestyle is necessary to save resources and they only use natural products (for example, cotton or wool clothes) and ride bikes instead of owning a car.

Evaluation of the scarcity of natural resources

To argue for the problem of resources being solvable, you could use the points from the possible solutions above. To argue against, you could use such reasons as:

- renewable resources for producing electricity are very expensive and will not work for many countries

- using plants for plastics and biodiesel is going to reduce the food supply, and people need food

- recycling is very expensive and uses a lot of electricity.

> **Common mistake**
>
> Students often think natural resources and renewable resources are the same, but oil, iron etc, are natural but finite.

> **Now test yourself**
>
>
> 1 What name is given to naturally occurring materials, such as oil and fertile land?
> 2 What name is given to resources which can be used over and over again, such as wind power and solar power?
> 3 What name is given to resources which disappear once they are used, such as oil, coal, iron and tin?
> 4 What could be used to power cars instead of petrol and diesel?
>
> **Answers on page 113**

Topic 8.2.4 Christian teachings on stewardship

Christians believe that God gave humans the **stewardship** of the Earth and its resources. The Bible teaches that Christians were given the right to rule over God's **creation**, but only as God's stewards, and they must treat animals and the land kindly.

Jesus taught that Christians have a responsibility to leave the Earth a better place than they found it (the parable of the Talents/Minas) and to make sure the Earth's resources are shared fairly. He also said they will be judged on whether they have been good stewards of God's Earth.

Their beliefs about stewardship affect Christian attitudes to the **environment** because the responsibility to be God's stewards and to leave the Earth a better place than they found it means that Christians should try to reduce pollution and preserve resources. Christians should show stewardship by working to share the Earth's resources more fairly and improve the standard of living in LEDCs (less economically developed countries). The belief that they will be judged on their behaviour as stewards means Christians should help the work of groups which try to reduce pollution and **conserve** resources.

However, Christians believe human interests come first; for example, shutting down a factory which causes pollution but employs 3000 people would not be a Christian solution.

Evaluation of Christian teachings on stewardship

You may be required to argue for and against following religious teachings on stewardship being the best way to solve the problems of the environment.

1 To argue for following religious teachings on stewardship being the best way to solve the problems of the environment, you could use the points above about how stewardship affects Christian attitudes to the environment.

2 To argue against religious teachings on stewardship being the best way to solve the problems of the environment, you could use such reasons as:

- only government action can deal with problems like the disposal of waste

- religion might change people's attitudes, but it won't build alternative energy producers such as wind farms

- recycling would have to be organised on an international basis, which would be difficult to do by religion.

Key terms

Stewardship – looking after something so it can be passed on to the next generation.

Creation – the act of creating the universe or the universe which has been created.

Environment – the surroundings in which plants and animals live and on which they depend.

Conservation – protecting and preserving natural resources and the environment.

Common mistake

When answering evaluation questions, make sure you give three reasons against your point of view otherwise you stand to lose 2 marks.

Now test yourself

1 Who do Christians believe gave humans the stewardship of the Earth and its resources?
2 In which parable did Jesus teach that Christians have a responsibility to leave the Earth a better place than they found it?
3 Who said that Christians will be judged on whether they have been good stewards of God's Earth?
4 How do Christians show their stewardship of the Earth?

Answers on page 112

Topic 8.2.5 Islam and stewardship

If you have studied either Judaism, or Hinduism or Sikhism at school, you can find the revision notes for these on the website: **www.therevisionbutton.co.uk/myrevisionnotes**

Islam teaches that God created Adam as his khalifah (type of steward). This means that all Muslims are God's khalifahs who have to keep the balance of creation and look after the Earth for God in the way set out in the Qur'an and the Shari'ah. Islam also teaches that people will be judged by God on the way they have looked after the Earth and the life on Earth. This life is a test from God and a main part of the test is looking after the environment in the way of Islam. Those who fail the test will be punished.

Their beliefs about stewardship affect Muslim attitudes to the environment because the responsibility to be God's khalifah means that Muslims should try to reduce pollution and preserve resources. The Shari'ah and Ummah tell Muslims that stewardship includes sharing the Earth's resources, so Muslims should work to share the Earth's resources more fairly and improve the standard of living in LEDCs. The belief that they will be judged on their behaviour as khalifahs means Muslims have a duty to help the work of groups which try to reduce pollution and conserve resources. Islam teaches that there is a unity and balance in creation, and therefore Muslims have a duty to preserve the environment.

However, Muslims believe that human interests come first and so the effects of environmental projects on humans cannot be ignored.

Evaluation of Islam and stewardship

Evaluation questions will ask you to refer to only one religion. It would be best just to use Christianity in answering evaluation questions, although you could use extra reasons from Islam.

> **Exam tip**
>
> When a question says, 'Choose one religion other than Christianity', always begin your answer with the words, 'I am choosing to answer on Islam …'.

> **Now test yourself** ———————————————————— Tested
>
> 1 Who did God create as his first khalifah?
> 2 Who has to keep the balance of creation and look after the Earth for God in the way set out in the Qur'an and the Shari'ah?
> 3 What is a main part of the test God intends this life to be?
> 4 Why do Muslims have a duty to preserve the environment?
>
> **Answers on page 113**

Topic 8.2.6 Medical treatments for infertility

Revised

The main medical treatments for **infertility** are as follows:

- IVF (**in-vitro fertilisation**): when an egg is taken from the mother's womb, fertilised in a test-tube and put back in the womb.

- AIH (**artificial insemination** by husband): when the husband's sperm is used for IVF.

- AID (artificial insemination by donor): when an unknown man's sperm is used for IVF.

- Egg donation: when an unknown woman's egg and the husband's sperm are fertilised by IVF.

- **Embryo** donation: when both sperm and egg are from unknown donors and are fertilised by IVF.

- **Surrogacy**: when either the egg and sperm of husband and wife, or the egg or sperm of husband or wife and an unknown donor, are fertilised by IVF and then placed in another woman's womb and the baby handed to the husband and wife after the birth.

All the medical treatments now being used by couples in Britain are supervised by the Human Fertilisation and Embryology Authority (HFEA). Since 1 April 2005, children born from donated sperm, eggs or embryos have the right to discover their genetic parents when they are eighteen years old.

Why infertility treatments are important

- As many as 12.5 per cent of couples in the UK have fertility problems.

- Up to 1.5 million men in the UK alone have fertility problems.

- In 2007, 12 per cent of all births in the UK were as a result of fertility treatments.

- It is a part of human nature to want to have children and raise a family, and psychological problems are caused if couples are desperate to have children but cannot.

Evaluation of medical treatments for infertility

Questions on infertility treatments will ask you to refer to at least one religion, so the advice on evaluation comes after Topic 8.2.7.

> **Key terms**
>
> **Infertility** – not being able to have children.
>
> **In-vitro fertilisation** – the method of fertilising a human egg in a test-tube.
>
> **Artificial insemination** – injecting semen into the uterus by artificial means.
>
> **Embryo** – a fertilised egg in the first eight weeks after conception.
>
> **Surrogacy** – an arrangement whereby a woman bears a child on behalf of another woman.

> **Exam tip**
>
> Remember to mention in your answers that IVF is involved in most infertility treatments.

> **Now test yourself** Tested
>
> 1 What treatment involves an egg being taken from the mother's womb, fertilised in a test-tube and put back in the womb?
> 2 What treatment involves an unknown woman's egg and the husband's sperm being fertilised by IVF?
> 3 What treatment involves the egg and sperm of husband and wife being fertilised by IVF and then placed in another woman's womb?
> 4 What percentage of couples in the UK are thought to have fertility problems?
>
> **Answers on page 113**

Topic 8.2.7 Different Christian attitudes to infertility treatments

Catholic Christians

Catholic Christians believe that life is given by God and that no one has a right to children, so only allow methods which do not affect the sanctity of life and in which sex acts are natural. Therefore all treatments involving medical technology are banned because:

● IVF involves fertilising several eggs, some of which are thrown away or used for experimentation; the Catholic Church believes that this is the same as abortion, which the Church bans

● all forms of artificial insemination or surrogacy involve the sin of male masturbation

● all forms of embryo technology involve fertilisation being separated from sex, but God intended procreation to be a part of sex.

Other Christians

Other Christian Churches allow IVF and AIH because:

● one of the purposes of Christian marriage is to have children, so infertility treatments must be good

● the baby will be the biological offspring of its mother and father

● they do not think the discarded embryos are foetuses and so life is not being taken.

They do not ban the other infertility treatments, but are worried because they involve problems about who the parents are and could lead to identity problems for the children in later life.

All Christians would encourage childless couples to adopt.

Evaluation of different attitudes to infertility treatments among Christians

You may be asked to argue for and against everyone having the right to have children.

1 To argue for everyone having the right to have children you could use reasons why infertility treatments are important from Topic 8.2.6 and the reasons other Christian Churches are in favour of IVF and AIH.

2 To argue against everyone having the right to have children, you could use such reasons as:

● infertility may mean that God wants the person to do something other than raise a family

● some treatments for infertility are against the teachings of religion

● some treatments for infertility cause problems about who the parents are and could cause identity problems for the child.

> **Common mistake**
>
> Students answer evaluation questions without referring to a specific religion. It is no use saying 'religious people' or 'religion' – you have to say Christian or Muslim.

Now test yourself

1 Which Christians believe that no one has a right to have children?
2 Why does the fact that IVF involves fertilising several eggs, some of which are thrown away or used for experimentation, lead the Catholic Church to ban it?
3 What do all forms of artificial insemination or surrogacy involve which Catholics regard as a sin?
4 Which Christians allow IVF and AIH because one of the purposes of Christian marriage is to have children?

Answers on page 113

Topic 8.2.8 Attitudes to infertility treatments in Islam

If you have studied either Judaism, or Hinduism or Sikhism at school, you can find the revision notes for these on the website:
www.therevisionbutton.co.uk/myrevisionnotes

Islam allows couples having fertility problems to use IVF and AIH because:

● the egg and sperm are from the husband and wife

● all Muslims should have a family

● the unused embryos are not foetuses so life is not being taken.

Islamic lawyers have banned all other infertility treatments because:

● they deny a child's right to know its natural parents

● egg or sperm donation is like adultery

● they are the same as adoption, which is banned in Islam.

Evaluation of attitudes to infertility treatments in Islam

Evaluation questions will only ask you to refer to one religion, so it would be best just to use Christianity in answering evaluation questions, although you could use extra reasons from the other religion you have studied.

Common mistake

Students often claim that Muslims are against all forms of infertility treatments rather than just some. Make sure to remember that Muslims are allowed to use IVF and AIH.

Now test yourself

Tested

1 Which fertility treatments does Islam accept?
2 What does Islam think egg or sperm donation is like?
3 What is infertility?
4 What is an embryo?

Answers on page 113

Topic 8.2.9 The nature and importance of transplant surgery

Transplant surgery is when organs are taken from one person and put into another person to replace an organ that is not working. A wide range of organs can now be transplanted successfully, from hearts to eye corneas. Transplant surgery is very effective and gives life and hope to people for whom there is otherwise no cure.

There are two types of transplant surgery – one uses organs from a dead person, the other uses organs from a living person which they can live without (for example bone-marrow, single kidneys).

In the UK, the Human Tissue Authority (HTA) controls **organ donations** so that people cannot sell their organs.

Transplant surgery is important because:

- it cures life-threatening conditions (like kidney failure) and improves people's lives (like giving sight to blind people)

- transplants save over 3000 lives a year

- more people need transplant surgery every year so transplants are essential

- transplant surgery gives people a chance to help others after their death by using organs which would otherwise be buried or burned

- it is pioneering surgical methods, which lead to the development of spare-part surgery (using artificial organs).

Evaluation of the nature and importance of transplant surgery

Evaluation questions on transplant surgery will require you to refer to at least one religion, so the advice is given after the next topic, but the information above might be useful for arguing in favour of transplants. If the organs of everyone who died in an accident could be used for transplants unless they had opted out, this could double the number of lives saved.

> **Key term**
>
> **Organ donation** – giving organs to be used in transplant surgery.

> **Common mistake**
>
> Students sometimes answer questions on transplant surgery as if there were no difference between live transplants and transplants from dead people and so do not understand the dangers of poor people selling their organs.

Now test yourself ———————— Tested

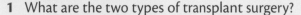

1 What are the two types of transplant surgery?
2 What organisation controls live transplants in the UK?
3 How many lives a year are saved by transplants?
4 What type of surgery is transplant surgery helping to develop?

Answers on page 113

Topic 8.2.10 Different attitudes to transplant surgery in Christianity

1 **All Christians** disagree with organs being bought from poor people because the Bible says the poor should not be exploited.

2 **Most Christians** agree with transplant surgery because:
- those who believe in immortality of the soul believe the body is not needed after death
- those who believe in resurrection believe that God will not need the organs to raise the body
- they believe that leaving organs for others is a way of loving your neighbour
- they believe leaving organs for others is a way of treating others as you would want to be treated and so follows the Golden Rule.

3 **Some Christians** agree with transplants using organs from living people, but not from dead people, because:
- they believe transplanting organs from the dead to the living is playing God, which is a great sin
- they believe that organs such as the heart are an essential part of a person created by God
- they think that donating your living organs is a way of loving your neighbour.

4 **Some Christians** do not agree with transplants at all and do not carry donor cards because they believe transplants:
- ignore the sanctity of life
- are a form of playing God, which is a great sin
- raise the problem of at what point someone is considered dead, and whether the surgeon saves the life of an unknown accident victim or the patient they know who needs a transplant
- take resources from less expensive cures which could help far more people than a single transplant.

Evaluation of different attitudes to transplant surgery in Christianity

You may be required to argue for and against Christians/religious people being involved in transplant surgery.

1 To argue for religious people agreeing with transplant surgery, you could use the reasons why most Christians agree with transplant surgery (part 2 above) and/or the reasons why your other religion agrees with transplants.

2 To argue against transplant surgery, you could use the reasons why some Christians do not agree with transplants at all (part 4 above) and/or the reasons why your other religion is against transplants.

Exam tip

Remember to make very clear in your answers that most Christians agree with transplants.

Now test yourself

1 What do all Christians think about organs being bought from poor people?
2 What do most Christians think about transplant surgery?
3 Why do some Christians not agree with transplanting organs from the dead to the living?
4 Christians who do not agree with transplants at all and do not carry donor cards believe that transplants ignore what?

Answers on page 113

Topic 8.2.11 Attitudes to transplant surgery in Islam

Revised

If you have studied either Judaism, or Hinduism or Sikhism at school, you can find the revision notes for these on the website:
www.therevisionbutton.co.uk/myrevisionnotes

Most Muslims do not agree with transplant surgery because:

- the Shari'ah teaches that nothing should be removed from the body after death
- they think that transplanting vital organs is playing God, which is the greatest sin of shirk
- the Qur'an teaches that only God has the right to give and take life
- transplanting organs is against Muslim beliefs on the sanctity of life
- they believe that Muslims need all their organs for resurrection on the Last Day.

Some Muslims allow transplants from close relatives because:

- some Muslim lawyers have said it is allowed
- the Muslim Law Council of the UK says that Muslims can carry donor cards and have transplants
- they believe that Islam aims to do good and help people.

Evaluation of attitudes to transplant surgery in one non-Christian religion

Evaluation questions will ask you to refer to only one religion, so it would be best just to use Christianity in answering evaluation questions, although you could use extra reasons from the other religion you have studied.

> **Common mistake**
>
> Students often mix up transplant surgery and genetic engineering and so give all the wrong information.

> **Now test yourself**
> Tested
>
> 1 What does the Shari'ah's teaching about what should happen to bodies after death mean for most Muslims' attitude to transplants?
> 2 What is the greatest sin for Muslims?
> 3 What Muslim authority says that Muslims can carry donor cards and have transplants?
> 4 What do Muslims believe they will need for their resurrection on the Last Day?
>
> **Answers on page 113**

Exam practice

Answer both questions

1 **a)** What is organ donation? (2 marks)

   b) Do you think religious people should support environmental organisations such as Greenpeace and Friends of the Earth? Give two reasons for your point of view. (4 marks)

   c) Explain why natural resources raise problems for humanity. (8 marks)

   d) 'If everyone were religious, there would be no environmental problems.'

      (i) Do you agree? Give reasons for your opinion. (3 marks)

      (ii) Give reasons why some people may disagree with you. (3 marks)

      In your answer you should refer to at least one religion.

      (Total: 20 marks)

2 **a)** What is global warming? (2 marks)

   b) Do you think the National Health Service should provide free infertility treatments for couples who cannot have children? Give two reasons for your point of view. (4 marks)

   c) Choose one religion other than Christianity and explain why some of its followers agree with transplant surgery and some do not. (8 marks)

   d) 'Science will solve the problem of resources.'

      (i) Do you agree? Give reasons for your opinion. (3 marks)

      (ii) Give reasons why some people may disagree with you. (3 marks)

      In your answer you should refer to at least one religion.

      (Total: 20 marks)

Summary

- Global warming means the Earth is getting warmer. Most scientists think global warming is caused by people putting too much carbon into the atmosphere, but some think it is caused by activity on the sun or by the nature of Earth's climate. Most scientists think global warming could be solved by producing electricity from wind, water, waves, etc, and by running cars on fuels which do not emit carbon.

- Acid rain (caused by the burning of fossil fuels) damages buildings. Human waste (refuse and sewage) and radioactive waste from nuclear power stations cause major health problems. Eutrophication caused by nitrates and sewage kills fish in streams and rivers, and litter dropped by humans leads to an increase in rat populations. These problems of pollution could be solved by producing electricity by wind, water, etc, using more efficient methods of waste disposal, recycling, nuclear reprocessing and geological storage.

- Non-renewable resources such as oil, natural gas and metals will run out, leading to major problems in our lifestyles. However, alternative energy supplies, recycling and using plants to make plastics could help solve the problems.

- Christians believe that God made humans to look after the world as his stewards. They have authority over animals and plants. However, the Bible also teaches that Christians should care for the environment and leave the Earth a better place than they found it.

- Islam teaches that God created humans as his stewards of the Earth. In the Qur'an he showed people how to look after the Earth. Muslims believe life is a test and God will judge them on how well they have looked after the world.

- There are now several medical treatments for infertility (when a couple cannot have a baby) such as in-vitro fertilisation (IVF), artificial insemination and egg and embryo donation. Infertility treatments are important because a lot of people have fertility problems.

- Some Christians, mainly Catholics, do not allow any of the fertility treatments because they involve either immoral sex or taking the life of unwanted embryos. Other Christians allow IVF and AIH, but are suspicious of all other methods even though they do not ban them.

- Islam allows IVF and AIH because they only involve the husband and wife. Islam does not allow any other forms of fertility treatment because they cause problems concerning the identity of the parents.

- Transplant surgery is using healthy organs from a donor to replace a dying organ in a patient. It is important because it can give life to dying people and it brings life out of death. Most Christians agree with transplant surgery, because they believe the body is not needed after death, but they do not agree with buying organs from poor people. Some Christians only agree with living transplants because using dead people's organs is 'playing God'. Some Christians believe that all forms of transplant surgery are wrong because it is 'playing God'.

- Most Muslims do not agree with transplant surgery because they believe they need all their organs for the Last Day. Some Muslims allow transplants from close relatives because it is allowed by some Muslim lawyers.

Section 3 Religion: peace and conflict

Topic 8.3.1 The United Nations and world peace

The **United Nations** (UN) was formed at the end of the Second World War to preserve **world peace** and bring about **conflict resolution** by encouraging economic, social, educational and cultural progress throughout the world.

The UN is important for world peace because, through the Security Council, the UN can try to stop any threats to world peace by:

- imposing sanctions on countries threatening world peace
- authorising the use of force by member states
- sending a UN peacekeeping force to prevent the outbreak of conflict, stabilise conflict situations and bring about a lasting peace agreement.

The UN also tries to keep world peace by running the International Criminal Court (ICC) at The Hague which upholds international laws and prosecutes anyone committing war crimes.

One example of the UN's work for peace

When Yugoslavia split up, Kosovo (an area with about 80 per cent ethnic Albanians and 20 per cent ethnic Serbs) became part of Serbia whose leader took away Kosovo's self-ruling rights. The Kosovars objected peacefully but failed to get any independence so in the mid-1990s the Kosovars began a guerrilla war. Serbia sent in the army and began a campaign of ethnic cleansing against Kosovar Albanians. Thousands of people died in the conflict and hundreds of thousands became refugees until NATO drove the Serbian forces out and the UN took over the administration of the Kosovo province of Serbia. Since 1999 the UN has protected Kosovar independence and the Serb communities in Kosovo. The UN then worked to set up political parties to allow Kosovar democracy to develop so that in February 2008 Kosovo declared itself an independent democratic state.

Evaluation of the United Nations and world peace

You may be required to argue for and against the United Nations being a good thing.

1. To argue for the UN being a good thing, you could use any of the ways in which the UN tries to keep world peace and/or its work with the International Criminal Court outlined to the left.

2. To argue against the UN being a good thing, you could look at ways in which the UN has not been able to prevent wars in such places as Syria, Somalia, the Democratic Republic of Congo, Darfur, etc.

Now test yourself

1. When was the UN formed?
2. What can be sent to prevent the outbreak of conflict, stabilise conflict situations and bring about a lasting peace agreement?
3. What body upholds international laws and prosecutes anyone committing war crimes?
4. What rights did Serbia take away from Kosovo that provoked the guerrilla war?

Answers on page 113

Key terms

United Nations – an international body set up to promote world peace and co-operation.

World peace – the ending of war throughout the whole world (the basic aim of the United Nations).

Conflict resolution – bringing a fight or struggle to a peaceful conclusion.

Topic 8.3.2 How religious organisations promote world peace

Revised

There are groups in all religions working for world peace such as:

- Christian Peacemaker teams
- Pax Christi International (a Catholic Christian group)
- the Muslim Peace Fellowship
- the Jewish Peace Fellowship
- Mahatma Gandhi Center for Global Nonviolence (a Hindu group)
- the Sikh Khudai Khidmatgar.

How religious organisations work for world peace

Religious organisations work for peace in the following ways:

- They organise meetings so that people learn about the horrors of wars and vote for political parties working for peace.
- They organise protests about war (for example, against the Iraq war and the Darfur conflict) to change public opinion and therefore governments' policy.
- They organise and attend interfaith conferences to help all religions work together to promote world peace.
- They work for economic justice and an end to the **exploitation** of poor countries by richer and more powerful ones. If the poor of the world had a decent standard of living there would be fewer wars.
- They work for worldwide acceptance of human rights to remove the causes of war. Many wars would be prevented if the governments of the world respected human rights.

> **Key term**
>
> **Exploitation** – taking advantage of a weaker group.

Evaluation of how religious organisations promote world peace

You may be required to argue for and against religious organisations doing more for world peace than anyone else.

1 To argue for, you could use any of the bullet points above about how religious organisations work for world peace.

2 To argue against, you could look at the work of the UN for world peace in Topic 8.3.1 and argue that it is more effective than the religious organisations.

> **Exam tip**
>
> When answering questions about religious organisations and world peace, make sure that you write only about religious organisations. Remember that the UN is not a religious organisation, it is a political one.

> **Now test yourself**
> Tested
>
> 1 What is Pax Christi International?
> 2 Who organises meetings so that people learn about the horrors of wars?
> 3 What would happen if poor people had a higher standard of living and there was more respect for human rights?
> 4 What is exploitation?
>
> **Answers on page 113**

Topic 8.3.3 Why wars occur

Religion

Wars often occur because of religious differences; for example, Serbia invaded Kosovo to protect the Orthodox Christians from the Muslim majority and in Kashmir the Muslim majority are fighting to leave India to become part of Muslim Pakistan.

Nationalism and ethnicity

Another major cause of wars is connected with nationalism and ethnicity; for example, the Tamil Tigers in Sri Lanka and the ethnic Albanians in Kosovo were fighting to have their own country. The civil war in Sudan is caused by ethnic and religious differences that were ignored when the country was established.

Resources

Wars can often occur because of arguments about resources; some people think that Iraq was invaded because the West wanted access to its oil reserves.

Ideals and politics

Wars can sometimes occur because of differences between ideals or politics. In the Democratic Republic of the Congo two different political groups are fighting each other for power. The UN is trying to bring peace but the conflict has become very serious. The Korean War began in 1949 when communist North Korea invaded capitalist South Korea. The UN sent a force to protect the South, and a truce was declared in 1953 but there is still no peace.

> **Exam tip**
>
> If you are asked to explain why wars occur, make sure you give at least four of the reasons on this page and do not write anything about where wars are occurring.

Evaluation of why wars occur

You may be required to argue for and against it being possible to end wars.

1 To argue for it being possible to end wars, you could use such arguments as:

- if religions came together in a search for peace and unity, religious wars would stop

- if we had a world federation of states (a world version of the EU or the USA), wars caused by nationalism and political differences would disappear

- if we had a fair sharing of the Earth's resources, economic wars would end.

2 To argue against it being possible to end wars, you could use any of the points above to explain why wars will never disappear.

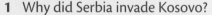

Now test yourself   Tested

1 Why did Serbia invade Kosovo?
2 Why were the Tamil Tigers fighting in Sri Lanka?
3 Why did the West invade Iraq, according to some people?
4 Who sent a peacekeeping force to protect South Korea?

Answers on page 113

Topic 8.3.4 The nature and importance of the theory of just war

Although most people agree that wars are bad because of their effects, most people also agree that some wars can be justified. The theory used to decide whether a war is justified is known as the **just war** theory.

Today it is generally agreed that a war is just if:

● the cause of the war is just (for example, it is fought in self-defence when another country attacks)

● it is being fought with the authority of the UN

● it is being fought with the intention to bring back peace

● it is begun as a last resort – all other ways of ending the conflict have been tried and have failed

● there is a reasonable chance of success

● the methods used avoid killing civilians

● the methods used are proportional to the cause; for example, it would not be just to use **weapons of mass destruction** to destroy a country because it had invaded a small island.

Evaluation of the nature and importance of the theory of just war

Any evaluation questions on just war will require you to refer to religion, and so they are dealt with at the end of the next topic.

Key terms

Just war – a war which is fought for the right reasons and in a right way.

Weapons of mass destruction – weapons which can destroy large areas and numbers of people.

Common mistake

Students sometimes claim the just war theory as being against any war or for any war rather than having strict rules about what type of war can be justified.

Now test yourself

Tested

1 What is the theory used to decide whether a war is justified?
2 Is a war fought in self-defence a just war?
3 Is a war fought with the authority of the UN a just war?
4 What are weapons of mass destruction?

Answers on page 113

Topic 8.3.5 Differences among Christians in their attitudes to war

All Christians believe that they are called to bring peace to the world.

Some Christians are **pacifists** and refuse to fight in wars. The largest Christian pacifist group is the Catholic Pax Christi. The Quakers, Plymouth Brethren and Christadelphians are completely pacifist Churches. These Christians are pacifists because:

- Jesus said Christians should love their enemies and turn the other cheek when attacked
- the fifth commandment says 'Do not kill'
- Jesus would not let Peter fight back when Jesus was being arrested
- modern warfare affects so many innocent people that modern wars can never be justified.

Many Christians believe they can fight in just wars because:

- it is the teaching of most of the Churches (Catholic, Anglican, Methodist, Baptist, URC)
- St Paul said that Christians have to obey the orders of the government, so Christians should fight in wars ordered by the government
- Jesus did not condemn soldiers – he actually praised the faith of a Roman centurion
- they believe that if we need a police force to protect innocent people against criminals, we need armed forces to protect innocent states against criminal ones.

> **Key term**
>
> **Pacifism** – the belief that all disputes should be settled by peaceful means.

Evaluation of differences among Christians in their attitudes to war

You may be required to argue for and against religious people being able to fight in just wars.

1 To argue for religious people being able to fight in just wars, you should use the reasons why Christians can fight in just wars given above.

2 To argue against, you should use the reasons for Christian pacifism given above.

> **Exam tip**
>
> If a question asks why there are different attitudes to war among Christians, give two reasons why some Christians are pacifists and two reasons why some Christians believe they can fight in just wars.

> **Now test yourself**
>
> Tested
>
> 1 What do the Quakers, Plymouth Brethren and Christadelphians think about war?
> 2 Who said that Christians should love their enemies?
> 3 What does the fifth commandment say?
> 4 Who said that Christians should obey the orders of the government?
>
> **Answers on page 114**

Topic 8.3.6 Attitudes to war in Islam

Revised

If you have studied either Judaism, or Hinduism or Sikhism at school, you can find the revision notes for these on the website: **www.therevisionbutton.co.uk/myrevisionnotes**

There is no idea of pacifism in Islam. The Qur'an encourages all Muslims to 'struggle in the way of Islam' (jihad). Muslims believe in two forms of jihad. The greater jihad is the struggle to make yourself and your society perfectly Muslim. The lesser jihad is fighting in a just war.

Most Muslims believe that if a war is just then a Muslim should fight in it because:

- the Qur'an says that Muslims must fight if they are attacked
- Muhammad fought in wars
- there are many hadith from Muhammad saying Muslims should fight in just wars
- the Qur'an says that a Muslim who dies in a just war will go straight to heaven.

However, some Muslims feel that the nature of modern weapons means that no war can be a just war, and so they oppose wars.

Evaluation of attitudes to war in Islam

Evaluation questions will only ask you to refer to one religion, so it would be best just to use Christianity in answering evaluation questions, although you could use extra reasons from Islam.

> **Exam tip**
>
> If you are asked to, 'Choose one religion other than Christianity and explain its attitudes to war', make sure to give at least three reasons why Muslims feel they should fight in just wars and then explain why modern weapons make some Muslims feel they cannot fight in wars.

Now test yourself

Tested

1 What is the struggle to make yourself and your society perfectly Muslim?
2 What do Muslims call fighting in a just war?
3 What says that Muslims must fight if they are attacked?
4 What do some Muslims feel the nature of modern weapons means?

Answers on page 114

Topic 8.3.7 Christian attitudes to bullying

Bullying is frightening people who are weaker than you. Most people connect bullying with school and school bullying can include:

- name calling
- pinching, kicking, hitting
- taking possessions
- ignoring people or leaving them out of games
- sending abusive texts or emails
- abusing people because of their religion, ethnic origin, appearance, sexuality or disability.

Christians are against bullying because:

- Christianity regards using **aggression** or violence without a just cause as sinful
- Christians believe people are a creation of God and made in God's image, so they should be **respected**; bullying is mistreating God's creation and so is wrong
- it is the duty of Christians to protect the weak and innocent (for example, the parable of the Good Samaritan), but bullies do the exact opposite and so must be wrong
- Jesus taught that Christians should treat anyone in trouble as if they were Jesus – no Christian would bully Jesus and so they should not bully anyone
- all the Christian Churches teach that Christians should protect human rights, and so they should not bully because bullying denies the victim's human rights
- bullying has harmful effects on society, and Christians should always try to make society better.

Evaluation of Christian attitudes to bullying

You may be required to argue for and against Christians having a duty to stand up to bullies.

1 To argue for Christians/religious people having a duty to stand up to bullies, you should use any of the reasons above for why Christians are against bullying.

2 To argue against Christians/religious people having a duty to stand up to bullies, you should use such reasons as:
  - unless you are very strong, standing up to bullies could make the bullies even worse as they might bully the person standing up to them
  - it is always better to use the forces of law and order to stand up to criminals (which is what bullies are)
  - it is more important for Christians to help the victim (the Good Samaritan didn't attack the robbers).

> **Key terms**
>
> **Bullying** – intimidating/frightening people weaker than yourself.
> **Aggression** – attacking without being provoked.
> **Respect** – treating a person or their feelings with consideration.

> **Exam tip**
>
> When explaining why Christians should be against bullying, make sure to give four Christian reasons and not the sort of general reasons that could be given by an atheist.

Now test yourself

1 Abusing people because of their religion, ethnic origin, appearance, sexuality or disability is a form of what?
2 Christians regard using aggression or violence without a just cause as what?
3 Which parable shows that Christians have a duty to protect the weak and innocent?
4 What do all the Churches say Christians should protect?

Answers on page 114

Topic 8.3.8 Attitudes to bullying in Islam

If you have studied either Judaism, or Hinduism or Sikhism at school, you can find the revision notes for these on the website: **www.therevisionbutton.co.uk/myrevisionnotes**

Muslims are against all forms of bullying because:

● Islamic society is based on respect between the members of society; bullies have no respect for the people they bully and so do not understand Islamic society

● Islam regards using violence without a just cause as sinful

● any Muslim who bullies a fellow Muslim is acting against the Ummah

● it is the duty of Muslims to protect the weak and innocent, but bullies do the exact opposite and so must be wrong

● Muhammad said, 'Every Muslim is a brother to every Muslim'; no one should bully their brother and so Muslims should not bully anyone

● all the law schools teach that Muslims should defend human rights and bullying denies the victim's human rights.

Evaluation of attitudes to bullying in Islam

Evaluation questions will ask you to refer to only one religion, so it would be best just to use Christianity in answering evaluation questions, although you could use extra reasons from Islam.

Exam tip

When the question says choose one religion other than Christianity, make sure to say you have chosen Islam and make sure all your reasons are clearly Muslim reasons.

Now test yourself

Tested

1 What is based on respect between the members of society?
2 Any Muslim who bullies a fellow Muslim is acting against what?
3 What did Muhammad say about brotherhood?
4 What teaches that Muslims should defend human rights?

Answers on page 114

Topic 8.3.9 Religious conflicts within families

Religion can cause conflicts in families in many ways:

1 Religions tell parents to bring their children up in the faith and make sure they become full members of it as adults, so if the children reject religion it can cause many conflicts. Parents worry that without religion their children will become immoral and that they will not see their children in the after-life.

2 Children wanting to marry a partner from a different faith cause conflict because there can be no religious wedding ceremony when a couple are not of the same religion. There's also a problem of which religion the children of the marriage will be brought up in, and parents can feel their children have betrayed them by falling in love with someone from a different religion.

3 If parents do not follow their religion very strictly, but their children decide to be strict followers, this can cause major conflict, for example if the child wants to have a low-paid job as a priest (minister), imam or charity worker, or joins a religious community and is not allowed to marry, or if the child criticises the parents about their lack of religion (e.g. Catholic parents using contraception, Muslim parents running off-licences, Hindu parents eating beef).

4 Moral decisions can cause major arguments within religious families, for example if a Catholic or a Sikh decides to divorce and marry someone else, if a couple decide to live together rather than marrying, or if a family member decides to have an abortion.

Evaluation of religious conflicts within families

You may be required to argue for and against religion causing conflict within families.

1 To argue for religion causing conflict within families, you could use any of the points above.

2 To argue against religion causing conflict within families, you could use such reasons as:

- religion brings families together as they worship together and have a social life together

- children brought up in a religion are likely to believe in it and so it won't bring conflict

- most religious parents respect their children's right to freedom of religion when they are old enough, so it does not cause conflict.

Exam tip

If you are asked to explain how religion can cause family conflict, make sure you explain four ways – children losing religion, interfaith marriage, children becoming more religious than parents and moral decisions.

Now test yourself

1 What makes parents worry that their children will become immoral?

2 What can make parents feel that their children have betrayed them?

3 Catholic parents using contraception, Muslim parents running off-licences, Hindu parents eating beef are all examples of parents not doing what?

4 What sort of decision is it if a couple decides to live together rather than marrying?

Answers on page 114

Topic 8.3.10 Christian teachings on forgiveness and reconciliation

Christians believe in **forgiveness** and **reconciliation** because:

● Jesus died on the cross to bring reconciliation and forgiveness

● Jesus said that if Christians do not forgive others, they will not be forgiven themselves

● St Paul said that Christians should try to live in peace with everyone

● all the Churches teach that Christians should use forgiveness and reconciliation to end conflicts.

However, Christians believe that a conflict about a moral or religious issue would not be able to be resolved. For example, if parents argued that a Roman Catholic son should not become a priest, the conflict could not be resolved because the Church would say the son must follow God rather than his parents.

Evaluation of Christian teachings on forgiveness and reconciliation

You may be required to argue for and against Christians having a duty to forgive enemies/bullies/those who wrong them.

1 To argue for Christians having a duty to forgive enemies/bullies/those who wrong them, you could use any of the reasons above for Christians believing in forgiveness and reconciliation.

2 To argue against Christians having a duty to forgive enemies/bullies/those who wrong them, you could use such reasons as:

● Christians cannot be expected to forgive those who hate them

● Christians should fight against evil and so they should oppose, not forgive, enemies/bullies/those who wrong them

● Christians are human and it is not natural for humans to forgive enemies/bullies/those who wrong them.

Key terms

Forgiveness – stopping blaming someone and/or pardoning them for what they have done wrong.

Reconciliation – bringing together people who were opposed to each other.

Common mistake

When a question asks why Christians, or one religion, believe in forgiveness and reconciliation, make sure you give four religious reasons and not just general reasons for forgiveness and reconciliation which even an atheist would agree with.

Now test yourself

Tested

1 For what reason do Christians believe Jesus died on the cross?

2 What did Jesus say would happen to Christians who do not forgive others?

3 Who said that Christians should try to live in peace with everyone?

4 What word means bringing together people who were opposed to each other?

Answers on page 114

Topic 8.3.11 Forgiveness and reconciliation in Islam

If you have studied either Judaism, or Hinduism or Sikhism at school, you can find the revision notes for these on the website:
www.therevisionbutton.co.uk/myrevisionnotes

Muslims believe they should be forgiving and try to bring reconciliation because:

- God is compassionate and merciful to sinners, so Muslims should also be forgiving
- how can Muslims ask for God's forgiveness on the Last Day if they are not prepared to forgive people?
- the Qur'an says that Muslims should forgive those who offend them
- Muhammad said in many hadith that Muslims should be forgiving.

However, Muslims believe they should not forgive those who work against Islam.

Evaluation of forgiveness and reconciliation in Islam

Evaluation questions will ask you to refer to only one religion, so it would be best just to use Christianity in answering evaluation questions, although you could use extra reasons from Islam.

Exam tip

When answering evaluation questions, if you are not religious, make sure to use at least three religious reasons for people disagreeing with you and make sure that it is clear which religion each reason comes from.

Now test yourself

Tested

1. As God is compassionate and merciful to sinners, what should Muslims be?
2. What will Muslims need to ask God for on the Last Day?
3. What says that Muslims should forgive those who offend them?
4. Who said in the hadith that Muslims should be forgiving?

Answers on page 114

Exam practice

Answer both questions

1 **a)** What is aggression? (2 marks)

   b) Do you think religion is the best way to bring about world peace? Give two reasons for your point of view. (4 marks)

   c) Choose one religion other than Christianity and explain why some of its followers believe they should fight in just wars. (8 marks)

   d) 'Religious people should always forgive those who wrong them.'

   (i) Do you agree? Give reasons for your opinion. (3 marks)

   (ii) Give reasons why some people may disagree with you. (3 marks)

   In your answer you should refer to at least one religion.

   (Total: 20 marks)

2 **a)** What is the United Nations? (2 marks)

   b) Do you think religious people should fight in wars? Give two reasons for your point of view. (4 marks)

   c) Choose one religion other than Christianity and explain why it is opposed to bullying. (8 marks)

   d) 'No Christian should ever fight in wars.'

   (i) Do you agree? Give reasons for your opinion. (3 marks)

   (ii) Give reasons why some people may disagree with you. (3 marks)

   In your answer you should refer to at least one religion.

   (Total: 20 marks)

Summary

- The United Nations (UN) was formed to preserve world peace. It is important because it brings all the countries of the world together and can send peacekeeping forces to stop conflicts. The UN sent a peacekeeping force to Kosovo to protect ethnic Albanians from the Serb army and has helped establish a democratic Kosovar state.

- All religions have organisations working for world peace by organising demonstrations against wars, educating people about the need for world peace and working for economic and social justice.

- Wars can occur for a number of reasons including religion, nationalism and ethnicity, and economic and political reasons.

- All Christians believe in working for peace, but some Christians believe that they should work for peace by refusing to fight in wars (pacifism) because Jesus taught Christians to love their enemies. Others believe the way to bring peace is to be prepared to fight in just wars because this has always been the Church's teaching.

- Muslims believe in peace, but Islam teaches that, if the faith is attacked, Muslims must fight a just war fought in a just way (jihad) because it is taught in God's word – the Qur'an.

- Christians are against bullying because Christians should protect the innocent and it is sinful for Christians to use violence without a just cause. Muslims are against bullying because they should treat all Muslims as their brothers and they should protect the weak and innocent.

- Religion can cause conflicts in families if children no longer wish to follow their parents' religion but the parents want them to, or if they want to marry someone of a different religion. Conflict can also occur if children become more religious than their parents and start criticising their parents or disagreeing with them over moral issues.

- Christians believe they should forgive those who attack them or hurt them and try to settle conflicts because Jesus taught forgiveness and reconciliation. Muslims try to forgive those who wrong them and try to resolve conflicts because this is the teaching of the Qur'an and they should forgive if they expect God to forgive them.

Topic 8.4.1 The need for law and justice

Revised

Law means rules about how people are expected to behave. The courts and the police make sure that all members of society obey the law.

We need laws because:

● people need to know what sort of behaviour to expect from each other; if there were no rules there would be chaos

● if there were no laws about business deals and work, modern-day society could not operate; people would not work if they weren't sure they would be paid and people would not make things if others could just take them

● we need laws to protect the weak from the strong; imagine if there were no laws on stealing, murder and rape – life would be 'nasty, brutish and short' (Thomas Hobbes)

● in an advanced civilisation, we need laws to keep everything organised.

There needs to be a connection between the law and **justice** because:

● if a law is unjust, people will feel that it is right to break the law

● if some laws are unjust, then they are not fulfilling their purpose of making sure that people are rewarded for their work, the weak are protected, etc.

● if a law is unjust, people will not obey it and will campaign against the law, causing trouble in society

● if the laws do not create a just society, people will think the legal system is not working and may start a civil war

● if laws are unjust, they will disrupt rather than unite society.

Evaluation of the need for law and justice

You may be required to argue for and against society needing laws.

1 To argue for society needing laws, you could use any of the reasons from the first set of bullet points to the left.

2 To argue against society needing laws you could use such reasons as:

● laws restrict human freedom and individuals should be free to do as they wish

● some countries have experimented with getting rid of traffic laws in towns and have found there are fewer accidents

● small societies work well without laws because people know each other and know how to treat each other without having any laws.

You may be required to argue for and against there needing to be a connection between laws and justice.

1 To argue for there needing to be a connection between laws and justice, you could use any of the reasons from the second set of bullet points to the left.

2 To argue against there needing to be a connection between laws and justice you could use such reasons as:

● the main thing is for everyone to know what the laws are; as long as people know what the laws are they can obey them whether they are just or not

● laws are there to help society to function; whether they are just or not does not matter as long as the laws work

● there is often no agreement on what is just, and some people may think a law is just while others think it is unjust.

Now test yourself

Tested

1 What is law?
2 Who makes sure all members of society obey the law?
3 What would happen if we had no laws?
4 When can laws disrupt rather than unite society?

Answers on page 114

Key terms

Law – rules made by Parliament and enforceable by the courts.

Justice – due allocation of reward and punishment/the maintenance of what is right.

Topic 8.4.2 Theories of punishment

If law is to work, there must be punishments for those who break the laws. In the UK, when someone is found guilty of a **crime**, a judge or magistrate decides the punishment. There are different theories about what punishment should do:

- **Retribution** is the theory that criminals should pay for their crime and their punishment is proportional to the severity of the crime committed. It makes criminals suffer for what they have done wrong – it actually punishes the criminal ('an eye for an eye').

- **Deterrence** is the theory that punishment should be so severe no one will dare to commit crimes. For example, if people know thieves have their hand cut off, then they will not steal; if people know murderers will be executed, they will not murder.

- **Reform** is the theory that criminals should be taught not to commit crime again. Many people think this is the best form of punishment because reformative punishments give criminals education and qualifications so that they can find a proper job and become law-abiding citizens (**rehabilitation** of offenders).

- Protection is the theory that punishment should protect society from criminals. For example, long prison sentences keep criminals out of society so that people and property are protected.

Most forms of punishment are a mixture of theories. Prison can deter, protect, inflict retribution and give reformation.

Evaluation of theories of punishment

You may be required to argue for and against retribution/deterrence/reform as being the best form of punishment.

1 To argue for retribution/deterrence/reform being the best form of punishment, use the relevant reasons given on the left.

2a To argue against retribution being the best form of punishment you could use such reasons as:

- applying retribution makes you as bad as the criminal because you are doing the same thing

- retribution will not stop criminals from reoffending

- retribution was condemned by Jesus in the Sermon on the Mount.

2b To argue against deterrence being the best form of punishment you could use such reasons as:

- people who are going to commit a crime do not think they will get caught and so will not be deterred by the punishment

- evidence from countries with the death penalty shows they have higher murder rates than countries which do not, and countries that cut off the hands of thieves do not have less theft (the poor steal to feed their families).

2c To argue against reform being the best form of punishment you could use such reasons as:

- reform does not work with many criminals as they re-offend

- some criminals, like psychopaths, cannot be reformed

- reform methods can be much more expensive than other forms of punishment.

Key terms

Crime – an act against the law.

Retribution – the idea that punishments should make criminals pay for what they have done wrong.

Deterrence – the idea that punishments should be of such a nature that they will put people off (deter people from) committing crimes.

Reform – the idea that punishments should try to change criminals so that they will not commit crimes again.

Rehabilitation – restoring criminals to normal, non-criminal life.

Now test yourself

Tested

1 Who decides the punishment for someone found guilty of a crime in the UK?

2 What is the theory that criminals should pay for their crime?

3 What is the theory that punishment should be so severe no one will dare to commit crimes?

4 What is the theory that criminals should be taught not to commit crime again?

Answers on page 114

Topic 8.4.3 Why justice is important for Christians

Justice has always been an important issue in Christianity because:

- the Bible says that God is just and will reward the righteous (another word for those who are just) and punish those who **sin**

- the Bible says that people should be treated fairly, and that God wants the world to be ruled justly

- there are many statements in the New Testament about how Christians should treat people fairly and equally

- all the Christian Churches have made many statements about the need for Christians to work for justice

- the Christian Churches organised the successful Jubilee 2000 campaign to persuade the governments of rich countries to cancel the debts of poor countries as they believed it was unjust (the Christian campaign for justice goes on under the name Jubilee Research)

- the World Council of Churches says Churches across the world should work for 'justice, peace and the integrity of creation'.

Evaluation of why justice is important for Christians

You may be required to argue for and against justice being more important for religious people.

1 To argue for justice being more important for religious people, you could use any of the reasons why justice is important for Christians given above.

2 To argue that it is important for everyone, not just religious people, you could use any of the points from why there needs to be a connection between laws and justice in Topic 8.4.1.

> **Key term**
>
> **Sin** – an act against the will of God.

> **Common mistake**
>
> Do not confuse the need for a connection between laws and justice with justice being important for Christians. Questions on why justice is important for Christians need Christian reasons, not the non-religious reasons on why there needs to be a connection between laws and justice.

> **Now test yourself** — Tested
>
> 1 What says that God is just and will reward the righteous?
> 2 What says that Christians should treat people fairly and equally?
> 3 Who organised the Jubilee 2000 campaign, as they believed the debts of poor countries were unjust?
> 4 What does the World Council of Churches say Churches across the world should work for?
>
> **Answers on page 114**

Topic 8.4.4 Why justice is important in Islam

If you have studied either Judaism, or Hinduism or Sikhism at school, you can find the revision notes for these on the website:
www.therevisionbutton.co.uk/myrevisionnotes

Justice is important for Muslims because:

● the Qur'an says God is just

● the Qur'an says that Muslims should treat people fairly

● Muslims believe it is part of their role as stewards of God's creation to treat all people fairly

● the Shari'ah is based on justice for everyone with everyone being treated equally

● Islam teaches that it is unjust to be involved in the charging of interest because it takes money from the poor and gives it to the rich.

Evaluation of why justice is important in Islam

Evaluation questions will ask you to refer to only one religion, so it would be best just to use Christianity in answering evaluation questions, although you could use extra reasons from Islam.

Now test yourself

1 What says that God is just?
2 How does the Qur'an say Muslims should treat people?
3 What is based on justice for everyone with everyone being treated equally?
4 Why does Islam think it is unjust to be involved in the charging of interest?

Answers on page 114

Topic 8.4.5 The nature of capital punishment

Capital punishment is punishment which takes away the criminal's life. This process is called the death penalty (execution). A crime which can be punished by the death penalty is called a capital offence. The UK abolished the death penalty in 1970.

1 There are non-religious arguments in favour of capital punishment such as:

- if people know they will die if they murder someone, it will put most people off murdering so there will be fewer murders
- murderers and terrorists threaten society and the best way to protect society from them is to take away their lives
- human life is the most important thing there is and the value of human life can only be shown by giving those who take human life the worst possible punishment
- retribution is a major part of punishment and the only retribution for murder is the death penalty.

2 There are also non-religious arguments against capital punishment such as:

- no court system can be sure that the correct verdict is always given; wrongly convicted people can be released from prison, but not if they have been executed
- statistics from countries with and without the death penalty show that, if anything, those countries which do not use the death penalty have a lower murder rate
- murderers who know they are going to be killed if caught are more likely to use violence to avoid being caught
- murderers often regard life imprisonment as worse than death, shown by the fact that they often try to commit suicide in prison (for example, Harold Shipman and Ian Brady).

Evaluation of the nature of capital punishment

You may be required to argue for and against capital punishment as an effective form of punishment.

1 To argue for capital punishment as an effective form of punishment, you should use any of the arguments in favour of capital punishment given in part 1 above.

2 To argue against capital punishment as an effective form of punishment you should use any of the arguments against capital punishment given in part 2 above.

Exam tip

In evaluation questions on capital punishment, only one point of view should be justified by the non-religious reasons in this topic. One point of view must be religious and give three religious reasons.

Now test yourself

Tested

1 What is another name for capital punishment?
2 What do some people think is the only retribution for murder?
3 Can any court system ever be sure to get every verdict right?
4 Which murderers tried to commit suicide in prison?

Answers on page 114

Topic 8.4.6 Different Christian attitudes to capital punishment

Many Christians believe that capital punishment is un-Christian, and that Christians should never use capital punishment when making **judgements**, even of murderers and terrorists. They believe this because:

- Jesus came to save (reform) sinners, but you cannot reform a dead person
- Jesus said that an eye for an eye and a tooth for a tooth is wrong for Christians
- Christianity teaches that all life is sacred, even that of murderers
- if abortion and euthanasia are wrong for taking life, so is capital punishment
- most Christian Churches have made statements condemning capital punishment.

Some Christians believe that capital punishment can be used because:

- the Bible gives the death penalty as the punishment for various offences
- the Roman Catholic Church and the Church of England have not cancelled their statements that capital punishment can be used by the state
- the Christian Church itself used capital punishment in the past for the crime of heresy (not believing official Church teachings)
- Christian thinkers such as St Thomas Aquinas said that the protection of society is a more important part of punishment than the reform of the criminal and they believe that capital punishment prevents murder and keeps order in society.

> **Key term**
>
> **Judgement** – the act of judging people and their actions.

Evaluation of different attitudes to capital punishment among Christians

You may be required to argue for and against capital punishment being acceptable to religious people.

1   To argue for capital punishment being acceptable to religious people you should use the points above on why some Christians believe capital punishment can be used.

2   To argue against capital punishment being acceptable to religious people you could use the points above for why most Christians believe capital punishment is un-Christian.

> **Common mistake**
>
> Students often claim that all Christians are against capital punishment and seem unaware of Christian countries like the USA having capital punishment.

> **Now test yourself**
>
> Tested
>
> 1   What did Jesus say about an eye for an eye and a tooth for a tooth?
> 2   If abortion and euthanasia are wrong for taking life, then capital punishment must be what?
> 3   Who said that the protection of society is a more important part of punishment than the reform of the criminal?
> 4   Who used capital punishment in the past for the crime of heresy?
>
> **Answers on page 114**

Topic 8.4.7 Attitudes to capital punishment in Islam

Revised

If you have studied either Judaism, or Hinduism or Sikhism at school, you can find the revision notes for these on the website: **www.therevisionbutton.co.uk/myrevisionnotes**

Islam allows capital punishment for three offences: murder, adultery and Muslims who abandon Islam (apostasy).

Most Muslims agree with capital punishment because it is a punishment set down by God in the Qur'an and because Muhammad made several statements agreeing with capital punishment for murder, adultery and apostasy. Muhammad also sentenced people to death for murder when he was ruler of Madinah. The Shari'ah says that capital punishment is the punishment for murder, adultery and apostasy.

Some Muslims do not agree with capital punishment because it is recommended by the Qur'an but is not compulsory. The Shari'ah says that the family of a murder victim can accept blood money from the murderer instead of death. They agree with the non-religious arguments against capital punishment (see Topic 8.4.5).

Evaluation of attitudes to capital punishment in Islam

Evaluation questions will ask you to refer to only one religion, so it would be best just to use Christianity in answering evaluation questions, although you could use extra reasons from Islam.

Exam tip

If you are answering the b) question and can't develop your reasons, give four reasons instead of two and you could get full marks.

Now test yourself

Tested

1 For which three offences does Islam allow capital punishment?
2 Who sentenced people to death for murder when he was ruler of Madinah?
3 Is capital punishment compulsory in the Qur'an?
4 Who does the Shari'ah say can accept blood money from the murderer?

Answers on page 114

Topic 8.4.8 Laws on drugs and alcohol and reasons for them

UK laws on tobacco

- It is illegal to sell cigarettes, cigars, tobacco, etc, to anyone under eighteen years of age.

- All tobacco packs must have large health warnings and shocking picture warnings about the effects of smoking.

- All adverts and sponsorship for tobacco products are banned.

- It is against the law to smoke in all indoor public places, workplaces, football grounds and all parts of railway stations.

UK laws on alcohol

- It is illegal to give an alcoholic drink to a child under five years of age.

- Children under sixteen can go into a pub with adult supervision, but cannot have any alcoholic drinks. However, children can be banned if the pub has had problems with having children on the premises.

- Young people aged sixteen or seventeen can drink beer, wine or cider with a meal, if bought by an adult and they are accompanied by an adult.

- It is against the law for anyone under eighteen to buy alcohol anywhere.

UK laws on illegal drugs

Class A, B and C drugs are termed as controlled substances and it is an offence to:

- possess a controlled substance unlawfully

- supply or offer to supply a controlled drug

- allow your premises to be used for drug taking.

The police have special powers to stop, detain and search people if they think they have a controlled substance.

Evaluation of laws on drugs and alcohol and reasons for them

You may be required to argue for and against having laws to control/ban drugs. As any such questions will require knowledge of the social and health problems caused by drugs, the advice is given after Topic 8.4.9.

> **Exam tip**
>
> Tobacco is a drug and so a question asking about the problems of drugs would include the problems of tobacco.

Now test yourself — Tested

1 How old do you have to be to buy cigarettes?
2 How old do children have to be to be given an alcoholic drink?
3 What are class A, B and C drugs known as?
4 Can the police search you if they think you have drugs?

Answers on page 114

Topic 8.4.9 Social and health problems caused by drugs and alcohol

Health problems caused by tobacco

Smoking increases the risk of various cancers, coronary heart disease, stroke, chronic bronchitis and emphysema. In men, smoking can cause impotence. The babies of mothers who smoke during pregnancy have a lower birth weight, are weaker and may not develop normally.

Health problems caused by alcohol

If you drink heavily, you have an increased risk of developing serious health conditions such as liver problems, stomach disorders, heart disease and some cancers. Heavy drinking can lead to alcohol dependence (**addiction**). About one in seven road deaths is caused by the effects of drinking alcohol.

Health problems caused by drugs

The physical health of users can be damaged by the toxic effects of a drug. Many deaths of drug users are caused by infections, liver disease or intentional self-harm. Heavy users often have psychological illnesses.

Social problems caused by alcohol

Alcohol causes social disorder in town centres, as seen on Friday and Saturday evenings. Other problems include:

- 41 per cent of all deaths from falls, 30 per cent of drownings, 25 per cent of boating deaths and 50 per cent of fire deaths are caused by the effects of alcohol

- 70 per cent of murder victims and 40 per cent of rape offenders had been drinking at the time of the incident

- 50 per cent of those who commit sex abuse crimes also abuse alcohol.

Social problems caused by illegal drugs

- Drug dealing often leads to violence between different gangs of suppliers.

- The high cost of maintaining a heroin or cocaine habit forces users into a life of crime. Some users become violent under a drug's influence.

- However, statistics show that the use of illegal drugs fell from 12.1 percent of adults in 1998 to 8.9 per cent in 2011.

Evaluation of social and health problems caused by drugs and alcohol

You may be required to argue for and against tobacco, alcohol and drugs being controlled by laws.

1 To argue for tobacco, alcohol and drugs being controlled by laws, you could use any of the points on this page about the health and social problems they cause.

2 To argue against tobacco, alcohol and drugs being controlled by laws, you could use such reasons as:

   - countries like the Netherlands have decriminalised some drugs and seem to have fewer drug problems

   - laws which prohibited alcohol use in the past, such as in the USA in the 1920s, caused problems with organised crime

   - it should be an individual choice as to whether to use tobacco, alcohol or drugs as they only affect an individual's body.

> **Key term**
>
> **Addiction** – a recurring compulsion to engage in an activity regardless of its bad effects.

> **Now test yourself**
>
>
> 1 What increases the risk of various cancers, coronary heart disease, stroke, chronic bronchitis and emphysema?
> 2 What are about one in seven road deaths caused by?
> 3 A large number of deaths from falls, drowning, boating accidents and fires are caused by what?
> 4 What often forces heroin and cocaine users into a life of crime?
>
> **Answers on page 114**

Topic 8.4.10 Christian attitudes to drugs and alcohol

All Christians are against drugs because they are illegal and they abuse the body, which is God's temple, so Christians have a **responsibility** to look after their body.

There are two different attitudes to tobacco and alcohol among Christians.

Key term

Responsibility – being responsible for one's actions.

1 Most Christians believe that the correct approach to alcohol and tobacco is moderation because:

- the first miracle that Jesus performed was changing water into wine at a wedding feast
- St Paul said that Christians could drink in moderation
- Jesus used bread and wine at his Last Supper and told his disciples to continue the tradition
- most Churches use alcoholic wine in their communion services, so Christians must be able to drink wine in moderation
- moderation is the teaching of the Catholic Church in the Catechism.

2 Some Christians (especially Pentecostals, members of the Salvation Army and many Methodists) do not drink alcoholic drinks and do not smoke because:

- they believe that taking tobacco or alcohol is abusing God's temple (our bodies) and there are passages in the Bible warning against drunkenness
- the Bible teaches that consumption of alcohol damages judgement, inflames passions and incites violence
- they are involved in working with alcoholics and so know how alcoholics need to be supported by others refusing alcohol (recovering alcoholics cannot have any alcohol at all).

Evaluation of Christian attitudes to drugs and alcohol

You may be required to argue for and against religious people drinking alcohol.

1 To argue for religious people drinking alcohol, you could use the reasons in part 1 above on why some Christians believe in moderation.

2 To argue against religious people drinking alcohol, you could use the reasons in part 2 above on why some Christians do not drink alcoholic drinks.

Exam tip

Make sure you give three religious reasons for each point of view when answering questions on Christian attitudes to alcohol.

Now test yourself

1 What are all Christians against because they are illegal and abuse the body?
2 What do most Christians believe is the correct approach to alcohol and tobacco?
3 Which Christians do not drink alcoholic drinks?
4 What teaches that consumption of alcohol damages judgement, inflames passions and incites violence?

Answers on page 115

Topic 8.4.11 Attitudes to drugs and alcohol in Islam

If you have studied either Judaism, or Hinduism or Sikhism at school, you can find the revision notes for these on the website:
www.therevisionbutton.co.uk/myrevisionnotes

Alcohol and drugs are prohibited for Muslims (haram) because:

- the Qur'an says that intoxicants are a means by which Satan tries to keep people from God and from saying their prayers
- the Prophet Muhammad said that every intoxicant is forbidden to Muslims (khamr)
- Muslim lawyers say taking drugs or alcohol is a form of suicide because you are harming your body, and suicide is forbidden
- Muhammad said several times that Muslims must not drink alcohol, and must also have nothing to do with the production or sale of alcohol.

Tobacco is regarded as haram by some Muslims because it harms the body, but Muslim lawyers have declared it makruh (disliked) because it is not mentioned by the Qur'an or Muhammad.

Evaluation of attitudes to drugs and alcohol in Islam

Evaluation questions will ask you to refer to only one religion, so it would be best just to use Christianity in answering evaluation questions, although you could use extra reasons from Islam.

> **Exam tip**
>
> A good way to answer a question on whether religious people should drink alcohol would be to use Christian reasons for arguing that they should and Muslim reasons for arguing that they shouldn't.

Now test yourself

1 What says that intoxicants are a means by which Satan tries to keep people from God and from saying their prayers?
2 Who said that every intoxicant is khamr for Muslims?
3 What do Muslim lawyers say taking drugs or alcohol is a form of?
4 What word do Muslim lawyers apply to tobacco to show it is disliked but not altogether banned?

Answers on page 115

Exam practice

Answer both questions

1 a) What is rehabilitation? (2 marks)

b) Do you think justice is important for Christians? Give two reasons for your point of view. (4 marks)

c) Choose one religion other than Christianity and explain the attitude of its followers to alcohol. (8 marks)

d) 'Punishment should be an eye for an eye and a tooth for a tooth.'

(i) Do you agree? Give reasons for your opinion. (3 marks)

(ii) Give reasons why some people may disagree with you. (3 marks)

(Total: 20 marks)

2 a) What is justice? (2 marks)

b) Do you think punishment should try to reform criminals? Give two reasons for your point of view. (4 marks)

c) Choose one religion other than Christianity and explain why some of its followers approve of capital punishment and some do not. (8 marks)

d) 'We don't need laws on drugs and alcohol.'

(i) Do you agree? Give reasons for your opinion. (3 marks)

(ii) Give reasons why some people may disagree with you. (3 marks)

In your answer you should refer to at least one religion.

(Total: 20 marks)

Summary

- Society needs laws for it to work properly and to protect the weak from the strong. The laws need to be just so that people will obey them and feel that they make society better.

- The main theories of punishment are:

  - retribution: criminals should be punished for what they have done

  - deterrence: punishments should be so harsh that no one would dare commit a crime

  - reformation: punishment should try to change criminals into law-abiding citizens

  - protection: punishments should protect society from criminals.

- Christians believe justice is important because the Bible says God is a God of justice who will reward the good and punish the bad at the end of the world. The Bible and the Churches encourage Christians to work for justice by campaigning for fair treatment for the poor, etc. Muslims believe in justice because the Qur'an says that God is just and the Shari'ah says Muslims must work for justice if they are to go to heaven on the Last Day.

- Capital punishment is punishment which takes the life of the criminal. Some people approve because it takes a life for a life and deters people from murdering others. Some people disapprove because there is evidence that it does not deter and trial mistakes can lead to innocent people being executed for crimes they did not commit.

- Many Christians think capital punishment is wrong because of the teachings of Jesus. Some Christians think it is right because the Church says it can be used to keep order in society. Most Muslims agree with capital punishment because it is the punishment for certain crimes in the Qur'an. Some Muslims do not agree with capital punishment because it is not compulsory in the Shari'ah.

- The law bans smoking in public and workplaces and says you have to be eighteen to buy tobacco. Alcohol cannot be sold to under-eighteens or drunk by under-fives. All classified drugs are illegal.

- Smoking can cause many serious health effects and deaths, which cause problems for families, employers, etc. Alcohol causes many health problems such as liver disease and alcoholism and major social problems as people behave violently and irrationally when drunk. Drug abuse can cause addiction and death. It also causes criminal gang problems and stealing to fund drug habits.

- All Christians are against drugs because they abuse the body, which is God's temple. Most Christians accept the use of alcohol and tobacco in moderation because this is the teaching of the Church; Jesus drank wine and wine is used for communion. Some Christians believe they should not touch wine or tobacco because of their harmful social and health effects and the Bible is concerned about the harmful effects of alcohol. Islam forbids the use of drugs or alcohol because they are banned in the Qur'an and in the hadith of the Prophet. Tobacco is disapproved of but not banned.

Glossary

Key terms for Unit 1

You must learn these terms for the exam as you have to answer four questions on them which are worth 10 per cent of the marks.

Abortion The removal of a foetus from the womb before it can survive.

Adultery A sexual act between a married person and someone other than their marriage partner.

Agnosticism Not being sure whether God exists.

Assisted suicide When a seriously ill person is provided with the means to commit suicide.

Atheism Believing that God does not exist.

Civil partnership A legal ceremony giving a homosexual couple the same legal rights as a husband and wife.

Cohabitation Living together without being married.

Community cohesion A common vision and shared sense of belonging for all groups in society.

Contraception Intentionally preventing pregnancy from occurring.

Conversion When your life is changed by giving yourself to God.

Discrimination Treating people less favourably because of their ethnicity/gender/colour/sexuality/age/class.

Ethnic minority An ethnic group (race) which is much smaller than the majority group.

Euthanasia The painless killing of someone dying from a painful disease.

Faithfulness Staying with your marriage partner and having sex only with them.

Free will The idea that human beings are free to make their own choices.

Homosexuality Sexual attraction to the same sex.

Immortality of the soul The idea that the soul lives on after the death of the body.

Interfaith marriage Marriage where the husband and wife are from different religions.

Miracle Something which seems to break a law of science and makes you think only God could have done it.

Moral evil Actions done by humans which cause suffering.

Multi-ethnic society One in which many different races and cultures live together in one society.

Multi-faith society Many different religions living together in one society.

Natural evil Things which cause suffering but have nothing to do with humans.

Near-death experience When someone about to die has an out-of-body experience

Non-voluntary euthanasia Ending someone's life painlessly when they are unable to ask, but you have good reason for thinking they would want you to do so.

Nuclear family Mother, father and children living as a unit.

Numinous The feeling of the presence of something greater than you.

Omni-benevolent The belief that God is all-good.

Omnipotent The belief that God is all-powerful.

Omniscient The belief that God knows everything that has happened and everything that is going to happen.

Paranormal Unexplained things which are thought to have spiritual causes, e.g. ghosts, mediums.

Prayer An attempt to contact God, usually through words.

Prejudice The belief that some people are inferior or superior without even knowing them.

Pre-marital sex Sex before marriage.

Procreation Making a new life.

Promiscuity Having sex with a number of partners without commitment.

Quality of life The idea that life must have some benefits for it to be worth living.

Racial harmony Different races/colours living together happily.

Racism The belief that some races are superior to others.

Reconstituted family Where two sets of children (stepbrothers and stepsisters) become one family when their divorced parents marry each other.

Reincarnation The belief that, after death, souls are reborn in a new body.

Religious freedom The right to practise your religion and change your religion.

Religious pluralism Accepting all religions as having an equal right to coexist.

Re-marriage Marrying again after being divorced from a previous marriage.

Resurrection The belief that, after death, the body stays in the grave until the end of the world when it is raised.

Sanctity of life The belief that life is holy and belongs to God.

Sexism Discriminating against people because of their gender (being male or female).

Voluntary euthanasia Ending life painlessly when someone in great pain asks for death.

Key terms for Unit 8

You must learn these terms for the exam as you have to answer four questions on them which are worth 10 per cent of the marks.

Addiction A recurring compulsion to engage in an activity regardless of its bad effects.

Aggression Attacking without being provoked.

Artificial insemination Injecting semen into the uterus by artificial means.

Bible The holy book of Christians, comprising the Old and New Testaments.

Bullying Intimidating/frightening people weaker than yourself.

Capital punishment The death penalty for a crime or offence.

Church The community of Christians ('church' with a small 'c' means a Christian place of worship).

Conflict resolution Bringing a fight or struggle to a peaceful conclusion.

Conscience An inner feeling of the rightness or wrongness of an action.

Conservation Protecting and preserving natural resources and the environment.

Creation The act of creating the universe or the universe which has been created.

Crime An act against the law.

Decalogue Another name for the Ten Commandments.

Democratic processes The ways in which all citizens can take part in government (usually through elections).

Deterrence The idea that punishments should be of such a nature that they will put people off (deter people from) committing crimes.

Electoral processes The ways in which voting is organised.

Embryo A fertilised egg in the first eight weeks after conception.

Environment The surroundings in which plants and animals live and on which they depend.

Exploitation Taking advantage of a weaker group.

Forgiveness Stopping blaming someone and/or pardoning them for what they have done wrong.

Global warming The increase in the temperature of the Earth's atmosphere (thought to be caused by the greenhouse effect).

The Golden Rule The teaching of Jesus that you should treat others as you would like them to treat you.

Human rights The rights and freedoms to which everyone is entitled.

Infertility Not being able to have children.

In-vitro fertilisation The method of fertilising a human egg in a test-tube.

Judgement The act of judging people and their actions.

Just war A war which is fought for the right reasons and in a right way.

Justice Due allocation of reward and punishment/ the maintenance of what is right.

Law Rules made by Parliament and enforceable by the courts.

Natural resources Naturally occurring materials, such as oil and fertile land, which can be used by humans.

Organ donation Giving organs to be used in transplant surgery.

Pacifism The belief that all disputes should be settled by peaceful means.

Political party A group which tries to be elected into power on the basis of its policies (e.g. Labour, Conservative).

Pressure group A group formed to influence government policy on a particular issue.

Reconciliation Bringing together people who were opposed to each other.

Reform The idea that punishments should try to change criminals so that they will not commit crimes again.

Rehabilitation Restoring criminals to normal, non-criminal life.

Respect Treating a person or their feelings with consideration.

Responsibility Being responsible for one's actions.

Retribution The idea that punishments should make criminals pay for what they have done wrong.

Sin An act against the will of God.

Situation Ethics The idea that Christians should base moral decisions on what is the most loving thing to do.

Social change The way in society has changed and is changing (and also the possibilities for future change).

Stewardship Looking after something so it can be passed on to the next generation.

Surrogacy An arrangement whereby a woman bears a child on behalf of another woman.

United Nations An international body set up to promote world peace and co-operation.

Weapons of mass destruction Weapons which can destroy large areas and numbers of people.

World peace The ending of war throughout the whole world (the basic aim of the United Nations).

Christian terms

These terms are useful as specialist vocabulary to improve your marks in c) and d) questions.

Anglican Member of the Church of England or those Churches in communion with it (known as Episcopalians in the USA).

Annulment A declaration by the Church that a marriage never lawfully existed.

Apostles Those chosen by Jesus to go out and preach his gospel.

Baptism Rite of initiation involving purification by water.

Baptists Members of evangelical Protestant Churches which believe in believers' baptism.

Bible The Christian holy book comprising the Old and New Testament.

Bishops Senior priests who are responsible for all the churches in a diocese.

Body of Christ A description of the Church.

Born-again An Evangelical Protestant phrase for personal conversion to Christianity.

Cardinal A specially chosen bishop who advises the Pope and elects new Popes.

Catechism A book summarising the teachings and beliefs of the Catholic faith.

Catholic A member of the Christian Church led by the Pope (often called Roman Catholic).

Church of England The official state Church led by the Archbishop of Canterbury and the Queen.

Creed A statement of Christian beliefs.

Denomination A group of religious believers who have their own organisation and faith.

Diocese A Church area under the direction of a bishop.

Encyclicals Letters sent by the Pope to bishops of the Church to teach or explain beliefs.

Eucharist A service celebrating the sacrificial death and resurrection of Jesus Christ using elements of bread and wine.

Evangelical Protestants Protestants who emphasise the sole authority of the Bible and the need to be born-again.

First Communion The first time a person receives the sacrament of the Eucharist.

Gospel The Good News about Jesus. Usually refers to the four gospels (Matthew, Mark, Luke and John) in the New Testament.

Homily A talk by a Catholic priest on how to apply the scripture readings in daily life.

Liberal Protestants Protestants who interpret the Bible and Christian beliefs in the light of reason and the modern world.

Magisterium The Pope and bishops being guided by the Holy Spirit to interpret the Bible and Tradition for Catholics today.

Mass The name given to the Eucharistic liturgy of the Catholic Church.

Methodist Protestant Christians who belong to the Methodist Church founded by John Wesley in the eighteenth century.

Minister A specially chosen (ordained) leader in Churches that do not have priests.

Moses The Old Testament prophet who led the Jews out of Egypt and received the Ten Commandments from God.

New Testament The second half of the Bible including the Gospels and letters.

Nonconformist A Protestant in England who is not a member of the Church of England.

Orthodox Churches Christian Churches which split from the Catholic Church at the Great Schism and which are in communion with the Patriarch of Constantinople.

Pope The head of the Roman Catholic Church.

Priests Specially called people who are ordained to lead worship and administer the sacraments.

Purgatory A place where Catholics believe souls go after death to be purified.

Quakers The Religious Society of Friends, a Christian denomination who have no sacraments and believe in pacifism.

Sabbath A day of rest and worship: Sunday for most Christians, Saturday for Jewish people.

Sacrament An outward sign instituted by Jesus through which invisible grace is given.

Salvation Army A Christian denomination founded by William Booth, known for helping the homeless and alcoholics.

The Sermon on the Mount Jesus' description of the Christian way of living found in Matthew's Gospel.

URC United Reformed Church formed by the union of English Congregational and Presbyterian Christians.

Muslim terms

These terms are useful as specialist vocabulary to improve your marks in c) and d) questions.

Apostasy Giving up or denying your religion.

Five Pillars The basic practices of Islam: Shahadah (witness), salah (prayer), sawm (fasting), zakah (charity tax), hajj (pilgrimage).

Hadith Sayings of the Prophet Muhammad.

Hajj Annual pilgrimage to Makkah, which is the fifth pillar.

Halal That which is permissible under Islamic law (especially referring to food).

Haram That which is forbidden by Islamic law.

Imam Prayer leader/community leader.

Khamr Intoxicants forbidden for Muslims.

Last Day The final judgement when the Earth will be ended by God who will judge everyone.

Law Schools The four Sunni and one Shi'ah interpretations of the Shari'ah.

Makruh Things which are disliked by Islam, but not totally forbidden.

Mosque Muslim place of worship, more correctly called a masjid.

Muslim lawyers Those who set out what Muslims can and cannot do in a particular country.

Prophet Muhammad The final prophet of Islam.

Qur'an The holy book of Islam.

Shari'ah The holy law of Islam.

Shirk The sin of associating things with God.

Six Beliefs The basic beliefs of Islam (belief in God, his angels, his prophets, his holy books, the Last Day and life after death).

Ummah The worldwide Muslim community.

Answers to Now test yourself

Unit 1

Topic 1.1.1, Page 1

1 They see people worshipping God

2 They take their children to church, send them to a Church school, teach them to believe in God and teach them to pray to God.

3 It keeps family together, gives a sense of belonging and an understanding of right and wrong

4 It can mean a lack of choice, a lack of freedom and can reinforce prejudices

Topic 1.1.2, Page 2

1 A way to contact God

2 A feeling of the presence of something greater than you

3 An event for which the only explanation is God

4 When your life is changed by giving yourself to God

Topic 1.1.3, Page 3

1 Design

2 Laws of science, DNA, evolution

3 Science

4 Destructive things like volcanoes and earthquakes

Topic 1.1.4, Page 4

1 The process of one thing causing another

2 That any effect has a cause and any cause has an effect

3 God

4 A cause

Topic 1.1.5, Page 5

1 15 billion years ago

2 Red Shift Effect

3 Laws of science

4 The Big Bang and evolution

Topic 1.1.6, Page 6

1 Agnosticism and/or atheism

2 Unanswered prayer

3 Not in the way we might expect

4 In the best way for everyone

Topic 1.1.7, Page 7

1 Because he is a loving heavenly Father

2 There would be no wars, no starvation, etc.

3 He would give what we need, not what we want

4 Answer prayers in the best possible way

Topic 1.1.8, Page 8

1 Free will

2 War, rape, murder, burglary

3 Earthquakes, floods, volcanoes, terminal illness

4 If God is both omni-benevolent and omnipotent there should be no evil and suffering

Topic 1.1.9, Page 9

1 God must have a reason for it

2 Free will

3 Paradise

4 He will reward the good in heaven

Topic 1.1.10, Page 10

1 Yes

2 Four

3 Four

4 Yes

Topic 1.2.1, Page 13

1 His resurrection

2 They say that Jesus rose from the dead and that there will be life after death

3 It says you will go to hell if you don't help the suffering

4 The unforgiven go to hell

Topic 1.2.2, Page 14

1 They believe it's God's word

2 So those who pass can be rewarded

3 They have to live a good life to avoid hell

4 Keeping the Five Pillars and food and dress laws

Topic 1.2.3, Page 15

1 When someone about to die has an out-of-body experience

2 Communicate with spirits of the dead

3 They are simply products of the patient's brain as a result of chemical changes

4 That the soul cannot survive without the body

Topic 1.2.4, Page 16

1 Judaism, Islam, Christianity

2 Mediums, near-death experiences, reincarnation

3 They contradict each other and there's no way of deciding which are true

4 It can't exist without the body

Topic 1.2.5, Page 17

1 Two doctors

2 24 weeks of pregnancy

3 At conception

4 When the foetus is able to live outside the mother

Topic 1.2.6, Page 18

1 Liberal Protestants

2 Life is holy and belongs to God

3 All abortion is wrong

4 Love your neighbour

Topic 1.2.7, Page 19

1 At 120 days of pregnancy

2 The mother's

3 Because it bans murder

4 It is allowed up to 120 days; it is allowed if the mother's life at risk; it is never allowed

Topic 1.2.8, Page 20

1 Providing a gentle and easy death

2 Stopping artificial feeding or not giving treatment

3 All types of euthanasia except passive euthanasia are murder

4 People who would have died are being kept alive with no quality of life

Topic 1.2.9, Page 21

1 Roman Catholics

2 Sanctity of life

3 Suicide

4 The Commandments ban murder and euthanasia is seen as murder

Topic 1.2.10, Page 22

1 The Qur'an bans suicide

2 Euthanasia is making yourself equal with God

3 It bans murder

4 If people use euthanasia they are cheating in the test

Topic 1.2.11, Page 23

1 They think media criticism can stir up religious hatred

2 It makes it close to blasphemy

3 Freedom of expression is a basic human right

4 A multi-faith society

Topic 1.3.1, Page 26

1 Cohabitation

2 New laws, increased gender equality, longer life expectancy and cheaper divorce

3 Increase in divorce and re-marriage

4 It gives them the same rights and treatment as an opposite-sex married couple

Topic 1.3.2, Page 28

1 Sex should only happen in marriage

2 The marriage vows, the Ten Commandments and Jesus' teaching

3 You can have sex without risk of pregnancy

4 Statistics

Topic 1.3.3, Page 29

1 They believe it is God's word

2 Sex should only take place in marriage

3 The marriage contract

4 The Qur'an and Shari'ah

Topic 1.3.4, Page 30

1 Death of a partner

2 That it's impossible because marriage can't be dissolved

3 It says divorce is allowed in the case of adultery

4 The effects of the couple not divorcing would be a greater evil than the evil of divorce itself

Topic 1.3.5, Page 31

1 It permits divorce if children are cared for

2 It permits divorce

3 That it's the most hated of lawful things

4 Because the marriage has often been arranged by the family

Topic 1.3.6, Page 32

1 One of the purposes is to raise a Christian family

2 As the basis of society

3 Leave their families to serve God

4 They see their family rather than religion as most important

Topic 1.3.7, Page 33

1 Treatment of family determines whether you reach heaven

2 That it's created by God as the basis of society

3 He married and raised a family

4 It brings children into the faith

Topic 1.3.8, Page 34

1 Roman Catholics

2 Liberal Protestants

3 Evangelical Protestants

4 Medical research

Topic 1.3.9, Page 35

1 It condemns it

2 Muhammad

3 Sex within marriage

4 Scientific evidence

Topic 1.3.10, Page 36

1 Roman Catholics

2 Almost all non-Catholic Christians

3 Catholic Church

4 Almost all non-Catholic Christians

Topic 1.3.11, Page 37

1 It is wrong

2 Because they do not allow abortion

3 Islam puts the mother's life first

4 Muslim lawyers

Topic 1.4.1, Page 40

1 Equal pay for equal work

2 The right not be discriminated against in employment on grounds of gender or marriage

3 Social attitudes, lower salaries and worse promotion prospects

4 Encouraged the introduction of equal rights for women

Topic 1.4.2, Page 41

1 Catholics and many Evangelical Protestants

2 Many Protestant Churches

3 St Paul

4 Because the priest represents Jesus

Topic 1.4.3, Page 42

1 In the home

2 The Qur'an

3 The Qur'an

4 Muhammad

Topic 1.4.4, Page 43

1 14 per cent

2 Racial prejudice

3 They begin to work against society

4 New people bring in new ideas and new ways of doing things

Topic 1.4.5, Page 44

1 Community cohesion

2 To get rid of discrimination and to build good relations

3 The 2005 London bombings

4 Riots and violence

Topic 1.4.6, Page 45

1 Parable of the Good Samaritan

2 St Peter

3 St Paul

4 Over 70 per cent

Topic 1.4.7, Page 46

1 God created the whole of humanity from one pair of humans

2 There should be no racism because all Muslims are brothers

3 The Ummah

4 Muslim leaders and local mosques work with other groups to promote racial harmony

Topic 1.4.8, Page 47

1 Mono-faith

2 To see what religions have in common

3 Children leaving their religion or marrying into another religion

4 Religious conflicts

Topic 1.4.9, Page 48

1 That believers should convert non-believers

2 A multi-faith society

3 Because state schools may tempt children into a different lifestyle and a rejection of their religion

4 The rights of parents to bring up children in their religion and the rights of children to choose their own religion

Topic 1.4.10, Page 49

1 Judaism, Christianity, Islam
2 Protestant Churches and Liberal or Reform Jewish synagogues
3 The National Framework on Religious Education
4 The Inter Faith Network for the UK

Topic 1.4.11, Page 50

1 Your choice
2 Your choice
3 Four
4 Four

Unit 8

Topic 8.1.1, Page 53

1 The Ten Commandments
2 They believe Jesus is the Son of God
3 How Christians should behave
4 The guidance of the Church

Topic 8.1.2, Page 54

1 Jesus working in today's world
2 Through the Church
3 The guidance of the Church
4 The Magisterium

Topic 8.1.3, Page 55

1 An inner feeling of the rightness or wrongness of an action
2 God
3 St Paul and St Thomas Aquinas
4 No one would know what sort of behaviour to expect from each other

Topic 8.1.4, Page 56

1 The most loving thing to do in the situation
2 Jesus
3 Love God and love your neighbour
4 It's God's word to Christians about how to live

Topic 8.1.5, Page 57

1 The Bible says nothing about them
2 The Magisterium
3 If their conscience told them to go against Christian teaching
4 The Bible or the Church

Topic 8.1.6, Page 58

1 The Human Rights Act
2 A fair trial
3 Religion and freedom to express their views
4 Go to court

Topic 8.1.7, Page 59

1 Because of the belief that life is holy and belongs to God (sanctity of life)
2 They believe all people are made in the image of God and are one human family
3 They believe that homosexuality is against God's will
4 They believe Christians should marry Christians so they raise a Christian family

Topic 8.1.8, Page 60

1 Eighteen
2 Income tax
3 National government
4 Local government

Topic 8.1.9, Page 61

1 The Golden Rule
2 The Sheep and the Goats
3 'Am I my brother's keeper?'
4 St John

Topic 8.1.10, Page 62

1 Cystic fibrosis, muscular dystrophy, Huntington's chorea
2 Cloning processes
3 Cybrids
4 The Human Fertilisation and Embryology Authority

Topic 8.1.11, Page 63

1 Liberal Protestants
2 Jesus
3 Roman Catholics and some other Christians
4 God

Topic 8.2.1, Page 66

1 The greenhouse effect (carbon emissions)
2 The troposphere
3 Solar activity
4 Wind, wave, nuclear energy, solar

Topic 8.2.2, Page 67

1 Acid rain
2 Eutrophication (lack of oxygen in rivers)
3 Radioactive
4 Waste problems

Topic 8.2.3, Page 68

1 Natural resources
2 Renewable resources
3 Finite or non-renewable resources
4 Water, sugar cane and electric batteries

Topic 8.2.4, Page 69

1 God
2 The parable of the Talents/Minas
3 Jesus
4 By working to share the Earth's resources more fairly and to improve the standard of living in LEDCs

Topic 8.2.5, Page 70

1 Adam
2 Muslims
3 Looking after the environment in the way of Islam
4 Because they will be judged on their behaviour as khalifahs

Topic 8.2.6, Page 71

1 IVF
2 Egg donation
3 Surrogacy
4 12.5 per cent

Topic 8.2.7, Page 72

1 Roman Catholics
2 The Church believes that this is the same as abortion, which the Church bans
3 Male masturbation
4 Non-Catholic Churches

Topic 8.2.8, Page 73

1 IVF and AIH
2 Adultery
3 Not being able to have children
4 A fertilised egg in the first eight weeks after conception

Topic 8.2.9, Page 74

1 Using organs from the dead and using organs from the living
2 Human Tissue Authority (HTA)
3 Over 3000
4 Spare-part surgery

Topic 8.2.10, Page 75

1 It is wrong
2 They agree with it
3 They believe it is playing God, which is a great sin
4 Sanctity of life

Topic 8.2.11, Page 76

1 They don't agree with them
2 Shirk
3 Muslim Law Council of the UK
4 All of their organs

Topic 8.3.1, Page 79

1 After the Second World War
2 A UN peacekeeping force
3 International Criminal Court (ICC)
4 Kosovar self-ruling rights

Topic 8.3.2, Page 80

1 A Catholic Christian organisation for world peace
2 Religious organisations working for world peace
3 Fewer wars
4 Taking advantage of a weaker group

Topic 8.3.3, Page 81

1 To protect the Orthodox Christians from the Muslim majority
2 To have their own country
3 To gain access to its oil resources
4 The United Nations

Topic 8.3.4, Page 82

1 Just war theory
2 Yes
3 Yes
4 Weapons which can destroy large areas and numbers of people

Topic 8.3.5, Page 83

1 It is wrong and they won't fight in wars
2 Jesus
3 Do not kill
4 St Paul

Topic 8.3.6, Page 84

1 Greater jihad
2 Lesser jihad
3 The Qur'an
4 No wars can be just

Topic 8.3.7, Page 85

1 Bullying
2 Sinful
3 The Good Samaritan
4 Human rights

Topic 8.3.8, Page 86

1 Islamic society
2 The Ummah
3 Every Muslim is a brother to every other Muslim
4 All the law schools

Topic 8.3.9, Page 87

1 Children having no religion
2 Children wanting to marry someone from another faith
3 Not following their religion properly
4 A moral decision

Topic 8.3.10, Page 88

1 To bring reconciliation and forgiveness
2 They will not be forgiven
3 St Paul
4 Reconciliation

Topic 8.3.11, Page 89

1 Forgiving
2 Forgiveness
3 The Qur'an
4 Muhammad

Topic 8.4.1, Page 92

1 Rules about how people are expected to behave
2 The courts and the police
3 Chaos – 'life would be nasty, brutish and short'
4 When laws are unjust

Topic 8.4.2, Page 93

1 Judges and magistrates
2 Retribution
3 Deterrence
4 Reformative

Topic 8.4.3, Page 94

1 The Bible
2 The New Testament
3 The Christian Churches
4 Justice, peace and the integrity of creation

Topic 8.4.4, Page 95

1 The Qur'an
2 Muslims should treat people fairly
3 The Shari'ah
4 Because it takes money from the poor and gives it to the rich

Topic 8.4.5, Page 96

1 Execution/the death penalty
2 Capital punishment
3 No
4 Harold Shipman and Ian Brady

Topic 8.4.6, Page 97

1 It is wrong for Christians
2 Wrong, as it takes life
3 St Thomas Aquinas
4 The Christian Church

Topic 8.4.7, Page 98

1 Murder, adultery and apostasy
2 Muhammad
3 No
4 The family of a murder victim

Topic 8.4.8, Page 99

1 Eighteen
2 Five
3 Controlled substances
4 Yes

Topic 8.4.9, Page 100

1 Smoking
2 Drinking alcohol
3 Drinking alcohol
4 The high cost of their addiction